ISABELLA VALANCY CRAWFORD
We Scarcely Knew Her

For John
Christmas 1995
from
Jean

Isabella Valancy Crawford

We Scarcely Knew Her

ELIZABETH MCNEILL GALVIN

NATURAL HERITAGE/NATURAL HISTORY INC

Published by Natural Heritage / Natural History Inc.
P.O. Box 95, Station O, Toronto, Ontario M4A 2M8

Canadian Cataloguing in Publication Data

Galvin, Elizabeth, 1926–
    Isabella Valancy Crawford : we scarcely knew her

    Includes bibliographical references and index.
    ISBN 0-920474-80-2

    1. Crawford, Isabella Valancy, 1850–1887-Biography
    2. Poets, Canadian (English)-19th century-
    Biography.* I. Title

    PS8455 .R63Z63 1994   C811'.4   C95–930203–4
    PR9199.2.C72Z63 1994

Design by Norton Hamil Design
Printed in Canada by Mothersill Printing (1988) Inc.

Natural Heritage/Natural History Inc. gratefully acknowledges the financial assistance of the Ontario Arts Council. The support of the Government of Ontario through the Ministry of Culture, Tourism and Recreation, and the assistance of The Canada Council are also acknowledged.

This book is dedicated to
Clare
with love

and also to
Catherine Crawford Humphrey
and
Isabella

CONTENTS

"A great poet dwelt among us and we scarce knew her."
John Garvin, 1905,
in his preface to
The Collected Poems
of Isabella Valancy Crawford

AUTHOR'S PREFACE

The afternoon of Friday, September 9, 1983 was warm in Peterborough, Ontario. Most women attending the Crawford plaque-unveiling wore summer dresses for the occasion. Some men removed their jackets.

A stiff wind rippled the usually calm waters of the Otonabee River and rustled through the willow trees edging the river banks of Scott's Plains Park. It whipped to life the flags arrayed behind the raised platform where dignitaries sat on a row of small, padded chrome chairs. It cooled the invited guests assembled on the park green, talking among themselves, waiting for the ceremony to begin. An R.C.M.P. officer in scarlet tunic stood at attention beside the platform, his face impassive. Poet Isabella Valancy Crawford 1850-1887 was about to receive official recognition and Peterborough, its first federal commemorative plaque.

Members of the St. John's Anglican Church choir resplendent in their red gowns, sang *O Canada*. Then, one by one, speakers rose to stand before the microphone: Dr. Edward Storey, member of the Historical Sites and Monuments Board of Canada; Alderman Roy Wood, representing the Mayor of Peterborough; local actress Rita Smith, reading a selection of Crawford's poetry; Senator Andrew Thomas, unveiling the plaque; and The Venerable

Keith McKean, former Archdeacon of Peterborough giving the benediction.

Scott's Plains Park had been specifically chosen for the unveiling. During the years 1869-1876 when Dr. Stephen Dennis Crawford and his family resided in Peterborough they had lived for a time in a terrace row facing the market square on Water Street immediately above the park where the T. Eaton store is now located. We were, in a manner of speaking, in Isabella's backyard. As well, a short distance away, where the river broadens to become Little Lake, a Celtic cross in the cemetery overlooking the water bears this inscription:

ISABELLA VALANCY CRAWFORD
POET
BY THE GIFT OF GOD

I had been invited to provide biographical information that day. As I stood before the microphone, I heard someone in the front row say: "Oh, good. Now we'll know why we are here!"

Had they not known? Well, that did not surprise me. How often had I heard the question: "Who was Isabella Valancy Crawford?" Despite the fact she is considered by many to be Canada's first truly *Canadian* poet, and despite the fact her work has been acclaimed by such literary luminaries as Northrop Frye, Desmond Pacey, A.J.M. Smith, James Reaney and Dorothy Livesay, people who really ought to know, still ask: "Who was Isabella Valancy Crawford?"

In 1905, John Garvin wrote in his preface to *The Collected Poems of Isabella Valancy Crawford*: "A great poet dwelt among us and we scarce knew her."[1] Passing years have done little to change this.

Penny Petrone expressed her frustration in researching the Crawford background: "Isabella Valancy Crawford's biography and literary career are recorded in a hodge-podge of histories, encyclopedias, newspaper clippings and occasional pieces of criticism."[2] Her opinion was reinforced by Dorothy Farmiloe: "The scarcity of verifiable facts, coupled with the many contradictory stories about her, makes the task of reconstructing her life difficult."[3]

Such contradictions are immediately obvious when existing Crawford family records are examined. The 1861 Census shows Stephen D., Sidney and Isabella born in Scotland, Emma in the United States, Stephen W. in Ireland, and Sidney R. in Upper Canada.[4] The 1871 Census has the whole family born in Ireland.[5]

Records at Little Lake Cemetery in Peterborough list the age of Isabella at the time of her death, February 12, 1887 as 34; while St. John's Anglican Church records show her age as 30. She was, in fact, 36 years old. It is now generally accepted that Isabella was born on Christmas Day in 1850. This date would agree with the 1881 Census, [6] and with a dated signature found on a manuscript in the Lorne Pierce Collection at Queen's University: *I.V. Crawford Dec. 2, 1868—age 18.*[7]

In 1902, Stephen Walter Crawford (Isabella's surviving brother) appointed John Garvin as literary executor. One would expect, because of Garvin's association with Stephen Walter, that Garvin and his wife, Katherine Hale, [8] would possess accurate biographical material. Unfortunately, this was not the case.

In a letter to Eliza Jane Crawford (widow of Stephen Walter Crawford) dated August 2, 1935 Garvin asked these questions:

1) Will you please tell me how many Crawford children died in Dublin while the doctor was absent

in Australia: also give me their sexes.
2) How many children altogether in the family?
3) Did any die in Paisley?
4) Was Isabella the 3rd, 4th, 5th or 6th child?
5) Was she older than the sister who died in
    Peterborough?
    [and in postscript]
    Do you know when Dr. Crawford died?[9]

Hale, in her book, had twelve children arriving in
Paisley.[10] Garvin did, however, in a later publication, cor-
rect some of the inaccuracies.[11] James Reaney's introduc-
tion to a reprint of the 1905 edition of Crawford's poems
contains much that is inaccurate. Particularly glaring is the
repeated reference to Paisley in Grey rather than Bruce
County.[12] Such are the contradictions and inaccuracies
that lead to confusion.

Isabella Valancy Crawford lived among us and we did
not know her, but she left a volume of poetry that
prompted A.J.M. Smith, poet and one of Canada's most
respected literary critics, to say: "*Malcolm's Katie* is the
first, and not one of the least, of the few poems that can
really be called Canadian, because its language and its
imagery, the sensibility it reveals and the vision it embod-
ies is indigenously northern and western, a product not of
England or the States but of Canada...With Isabella
Valancy Crawford the early period of Canadian poetry
comes to an end. Maturity had been achieved."[13]

From his far wigwam sprang the strong North Wind
And rushed with war-cry down the steep ravines,
And wrestled with the giants of the woods;
And with his ice-club beat the swelling crests
of the deep watercourses into death;
And with his chill foot froze the whirling leaves

Of dun and gold and fire in icy banks;
And smote the tall reeds to the hardened earth,
And sent his whistling arrows o'er the plains,
Scattering the lingering herds; and sudden paused,
When he had frozen all the running streams,
And hunted with his war-cry all the things
That breathed about the woods, or roamed the bleak
Bare prairies swelling to the mournful sky.

Malcolm's Katie, Part IV
lines 1-14

I was brought to the writing of this book by a series of related incidents. It all began in 1971 when Sharon Murphy, a niece of mine, shared a table in an airport lounge with Canadian poet Dorothy Livesay. As a result of their conversation, Dorothy Livesay wrote to me and asked me to search Peterborough Little Lake Cemetery records for information concerning the Crawford burial plot. I did.

Later that year Ms. Livesay and Penny Petrone (at that time working on her doctoral dissertation) [14] came to Peterborough and to my home. I was to visit Ireland. Would I see what I could find while in Dublin? Yes, of course.

Subsequently a visit to the Four Courts Building in Dublin and the wonderful discovery: Crawford, Stephen Esq. 'Thornberry' Bushfield Avenue, Donnybrook; and III Grafton Street—Crawford, Stephen and Henry, agents to The British Commercial Insurance Co. 1841. [15]

My interest in Isabella Valancy Crawford became known. A book was to be written by Peterborough women about Peterborough women. Would I contribute a piece? Yes, I would. *Portraits* [16] was published and contained my article, 'Isabella Valancy Crawford—Poet'.

Several years passed. A Kawartha Conference was

planned at Trent University. I was on the steering committee. There was to be a Crawford session. Would I contribute? Yes, I would. *Isabella Valancy Crawford—Poet By the Gift of God* became a video production.[17] Even now, I am not certain how this evolved. But there were several trips to the Celtic tombstone where I sat, meditated and communed: Help Isabella, help!

With the assistance of some people caught up in the spirit of the project, problems were resolved.

Following the Kawartha Conference various groups and organizations asked to see the video. Then, in 1983 I was invited to give the historical background at the Crawford plaque unveiling.

Several more years passed and a film company arrived in Peterborough to do a sequence for the T.V. series *Sketches of Our Town*. The producer-director, aware of Crawford and the fact that she was buried in Little Lake Cemetery, was informed of my interest in the poet. Would I do a camera interview? Yes, I would.

In 1987 the Peterborough Branch of the Canadian Authors Association wished to commemorate the 100th anniversary of Crawford's death. Could I come up with a programme? Yes, I could. *Obituary*, a monodrama was performed at the Peterborough Art Gallery and at the Peterborough Centennial Museum.[18]

Then Barry Penhale, Publisher of Natural Heritage, Natural History asked me to prepare a manuscript: nothing academic, as much biography as possible, photographs, a selection of her poetry—that sort of thing—a small book, something that would appeal to the general public, to the schools.

I began to work on my little book. Finally the manuscript was finished, mailed—and returned. They wanted more of her poetry in the main text, more of myself, less speculation, more investigation. Could I *find her* in her

work? Would I rewrite? No, I wouldn't. No, I couldn't. I
was tired of Isabella Valancy Crawford.

Then, what is this that follows?

It is what *I know* of Isabella. It is the sum total of my
knowledge of this poet whose memory plagues me so
much I am compelled to write about her. For whatever
reason, and so fortuitously, I have found myself, on sever-
al occasions in the right place at the right time. I have
been allowed to wander through, and photograph
Thornberry in Dublin, the little house in Paisley, the beau-
tiful Strickland home in Lakefield, the house in
Peterborough where Dr. Crawford died, and the never-to-
be-forgotten third-floor rooms where Isabella lived out
her last days in Toronto.

This account is not a critical analysis of her work and
no literary comparisons will be made. My purpose is to
present—not to interpret!

Elizabeth McNeill Galvin

ACKNOWLEDGMENTS

I am primarily indebted to Catherine Crawford Humphrey of Kelowna, British Columbia, grandniece of Isabella Valancy Crawford and granddaughter of Stephen Walter, the poet's brother. Through extensive research Mrs. Humphrey compiled information regarding the poet and her family. I have corresponded with Catherine Humphrey for many years and now she has graciously allowed me the use of her material.

I am also indebted to Daniel Shanahan of Dublin, Ireland who, on my behalf, researched the Crawfords of Dublin and found proof of Stephen Dennis Crawford's venture into jurisprudence.

Eric Parker of Paisley, Ontario, generously shared his knowledge of the Crawfords' first years in Canada, took me on a tour of the area and provided me with a copy of the commemorative issue of the *Paisley Advocate*, February 20, 1890.

I wish to acknowledge the cooperation of Joan Arnold, Walkerton Land and Registry Office; Donna Beal, Archives Assistant, Mount Allison University; Dale Cameron, National Archives; Bernadine Dodge, Chief Archivist, Trent University; June Fordham, Hamilton Public Library, Anne Goddard, National Archives; Marianne MacKenzie, Archivist, Peterborough Centennial

Museum; Christine Mosser, Librarian, Metro Toronto Library; Ruth A.M. Pearce, Librarian, Royal College of Surgeons of England; Leon Warmski, Archivist, Archives of Ontario; and the staff of Douro Township Office and the Peterborough Public Library.

Also my thanks to Margaret Parker, University of Toronto Press, Mr. and Mrs. Gordon Blake, and Susan Twist of Lakefield, Ontario; Jean Brien, Fern Doyle, Elizabeth Farquharson, Patricia Johnson, Martha Kidd, Margaret McCulloch and Dorothy Mutter of Peterborough; and Professors Gordon Johnston and Michael Peterman, English Department, Trent University.

Most of all, a special *thank you* to my husband Clare, for his help and encouragement, and for providing me with a Florida retreat to finally get this manuscript together.

ISABELLA VALANCY CRAWFORD
We Scarcely Knew Her

One

DUBLIN

By the eighteenth century Dublin ranked as the second most important city in the British Empire. Its wide streets and quays accommodated its elegant Georgian architecture including the magnificent Bank of Ireland, the Customs House, Trinity College and Four Courts Building. With its twenty-seven acre park, St. Stephen's Green, in the city centre and its cathedrals and its theatres Dublin was indeed a sophisticated lady.

The Crawford family were at home in this setting. Originally from Cunningburne, Scotland, William Crawford settled in County Antrim about 1616. His descendant, Stephen Crawford, married Anne Dennis, daughter of the Reverend John Dennis, Rector of Kilkerrin in the County of Galway. It is not known precisely when they took up residence in Dublin, but Stephen Crawford's name was recorded in the Voters' Lists 1836-1845[1] with the address given as *Thornberry*, Bushfield Avenue, Donnybrook, Dublin. His business address was 111 Grafton Street where he and Henry Crawford were listed as agents for the British Commercial Insurance Company.[2]

Stephen and Anne had four sons: William, Stephen Dennis, Henry and John Irwin. William, the eldest, was born March 12, 1805 and educated in London and Dublin to become a barrister. Henry Crawford was born July 31, 1809 and was admitted to the Irish Bar in 1840. He married Elizabeth Larkan of Roscommon and is known to have had two children, Henry Dennis and Anne Philippa.[3] He was listed in the Dublin Almanac 1841 in partnership with his father, Stephen, as an agent for the British Commercial Insurance Company at 111 Grafton Street. John Irwin Crawford, born in 1812, became a staff surgeon in the Royal Navy and did not marry.

And then there was Stephen Dennis Crawford, born in 1807, father of Isabella, educated to become—what?

When I began my research of the Crawford saga, it was known that a Dr. Stephen Dennis Crawford had emigrated to Canada, with the credentials M.D., M.R.C.S. England. At that time, in order to practice medicine in Upper Canada, it was only necessary for Dr. Crawford to take an oath before a judge that he was the person named in the certificate presented.

Information received later from the Law Library of The General Council of The Bar of Ireland revealed Stephen Dennis Crawford was also a law student:

> Stephen Dennis Crawford. Son of Stephen of Grafton Street, Dublin. Under 34 years of age at the time of entering King's Inns. (due process in pursuing a legal career)
>
> Education in Dublin and Edinburgh. Formerly a surgeon. Entered King's Inns Hilary Term 1842.

It is reasonable to assume the Crawford family was affluent. The sons were well educated. William and Henry were married in St. Andrew's Church in what was, at the time, the wealthy parish of St. Andrew's[4]. They were believed to have had apartment's above their place of business on Grafton Street, and they had a country home *Thornberry* in fashionable Donnybrook.

I had an opportunity to see *Thornberry* in December 1989. My husband and I were in Ireland for Christmas, and in Dublin for a few days. Bushfield Avenue had been renamed Malborough Road. I knew the address was No. 55 and I had photographs of the house, but I did not dream that I would be allowed inside. We drove slowly along Malborough Road, and suddenly there it was, set back from the street behind an iron fence. Even our cab driver became excited. The building was now owned and occupied by the Carmelite Order of Priests. When I knocked at the front door, Father Michael McGoldrick greeted me. I had with me a copy of the Kawartha Conference publication which I gave to him, as it contained a photography of *Thornberry* and I explained my mission, pilgrimage really, but I did not use that term while talking with the Father. We toured the house which now encompassed No. 53 Malborough Road as well as No. 55, something that had not been previously known. He pointed out the carriage-way and we walked into the back walled garden where he showed me the original stone walls. No. 53 had been renovated, but the rooms of what comprised No. 55 were much as they had been in the 1840s with wide halls, high ceilings, thick walls to accommodate the numerous fireplaces, ten, if not more, and at least fourteen rooms. "It would have been, for the time, a fairly grand house," explained Father McGoldrick.

Exactly when Stephen Dennis Crawford married Sydney Scott of Cork is not known. Where they lived in Dublin has yet to be discovered. When Dr. Crawford was admitted to the King's Inns in Dublin in 1842 aspiring to a legal career, records state he was "a former surgeon" educated in Dublin and Edinburgh. In actuality, his attendance at Edinburgh University consisted of one class in clinical medicine in the winter of 1832-33.[5]

The 1845 Annual Report of Coombe-Lying-In Hospital in Dublin listed Stephen Crawford as a Medical Practitioner who had attended a full Course of Practical Midwifery and received the customary diploma. It is impossible to tell in what year Stephen Crawford received this diploma as all persons who had qualified from the time the hospital first opened in 1826 were listed.

In correspondence with The Royal College of Surgeons of England I was told:

"...I can verify for you that Stephen Dennis Crawford became a Member of the Royal College of Surgeons on 22 January 1836. His name appears in the lists from 1836 until 1842 (which also states that he is a surgeon for the East India Company)—from 1843 to 1849 he is mentioned in the section for those who have not returned the annual circular—, he is not mentioned after 1850.... He was a surgeon for the East India Company sometime between 1836 and 1842 when he returned to Ireland—which would coincide with him not returning his circular to the College from which the Members Lists were compiled. It thus seems perfectly reasonable that he would describe himself as a "former surgeon". The only other reference we have pertaining to this man is in the 1845 Medical Directory—in which he is listed as a Member of this College. (I might add that this edition was the first so all members whether or not they were practicing were probably included—he does not appear in later editions).

...It also might explain the discrepancy in many letters we have received here in the Library which call Stephen a 'Dr.'. There is a very clear difference between a surgeon and a physician, the latter usually being the holder of a University Doctorate which entitled him to the use of 'Dr.' before his name."

And so it would seem Stephen Dennis Crawford did indeed belong to the Royal College of Surgeons of England, though it appears that it does not necessarily follow that he was entitled to use M.D. after his name. This information only further confounds the question of his legitimacy as a medical practitioner in the Province of Ontario.

What we do know is, that in the year 1850 on Christmas Day in the city of Dublin, Sydney Scott Crawford gave birth to a baby girl. She and her husband, Stephen Dennis Crawford, named their sixth child, Isabella Valancy.[6] Years later Isabella would write:

I am of mingld (sic) Scotch, French and English descent, born in Dublin, Ireland. My father was Stephen Dennis Crawford, M.D., M.R.C.S. England, and L.M.B.U. Canada. I am his sixth child and only surviving daughter. I was brought to Canada by my parents in my earliest childhood, and have never left the country since that period. I was educated at home, and have never left my home but for about a month, that amount of absence being scattered over all my life. My father settled in Peterborough, Ontario where he passed out. My mother and I came then to Toronto, where we have ever since resided. I have written largely for the American Press, but only published one volume on my own account "Old Spookses' Pass, Malcolm's Katie and Other Poems" which appeared in 1884, in Toronto, and is decorated with press errors as a Zulu chief is laden with beads. Voila tout!"[7]

Well, it wasn't ALL, but that was how Isabella summarized her life in 1885.

In her autobiographical sketch Isabella stated she was of "mingld Scotch, French and English descent." There is no mention of an Irish heritage, and this is curious considering the fact she was born in Dublin, and that her father's family had been in Ireland for over two hundred years. Not so puzzling, however, when one realizes the Anglo-Irish considered themselves British, not Irish.

And yet this not-so-Irish poet grieved for Ireland in her bitter struggle with England for home rule and survival:

> Sons, for ages I have sat
> Sackcloth-girded on the ground,
> Glory-widowed, captive queen,
> Shackled, dethroned and discrowned;
> Mute my harp, ingloriously
> Dumb its old heroic strains;
> But its loosened strings wailed low,
> Vibrant to my clanking chains.
>
> Erin's Warning
lines 9-18

In September 1845 the potato blight re-appeared in Ireland, and 'the Great Famine' swept through the land. In the summer of 1847 it was calculated that three million people were kept alive by charity.[8]

> But 'twas the year the praties felt the rain,
> An' rotted in the soil; an' just to dhraw
> The breath of life was one long hungry pain.
> ...An' och the sod was green that summer's day
> An' rainbows crossed the low hills, blue an' fair;
> But black an' foul the blighted furrows stretched,

An' sent their cruel poison through the air.

A Hungry Day
lines 10 - 13
and 37 - 40

Ireland was struggling during these years to survive political unrest as well as the ravages of famine and fever. Hundreds of thousands of Ireland's population emigrated to other lands. The Crawford brothers all felt the lure of distant lands. John Irwin, as a surgeon in the Royal Navy, served on a number of ships around the globe, while the eldest son William, emigrated to Bombay as a barrister.[9]

The known facts of the Stephen Dennis Crawford family background are isolated, broken slivers and bits of information. Yet, from what is available, it is possible to piece together some of the fragments. One such fragment is the existence of a cemetery record in Peterborough, Ontario, which states that daughter Emma Naomi was born in Wisconsin in 1854. It would seem safe to say that Dr. Crawford and his wife were there at the time, though it is questionable as to whether they would have travelled with all their children. Why were they there? Was Dr. Crawford looking for a place to practice law?—or medicine?

In 1855, Dr. Crawford sailed for Australia to investigate the possibilities of that land.[10] While he was away, he left his family in the care of his brother, Henry, in Dublin. Tragedy struck! The Crawford children had been able to avoid famine, but with fever it was a different story. In one week seven of the doctor's eleven children became ill and died. How the mother, Mrs. Crawford, could endure such a loss is difficult to understand, but she did.

Who curseth Sorrow knows her not at all.
Dark matrix she, from which the human soul

Has its last birth.
..Without the loud, deep clamour of her wail,
The iron of her hands, the biting brine
Of her black tears, the soul, but lightly built
Of indeterminate spirit, like a mist
Would lapse to chaos in soft, gilded dreams
As mists fade in the gazing of the sun.

Malcolm's Katie Part VI
lines 1-3
and 7-12

Dr. Crawford returned from Australia and once again
Sydney Scott Crawford was "with child". A son, Stephen
Walter, was born December 25, 1856. The story is told
that his head was so small it could fit into a tea cup. "He
was baptized in the [Roman] Catholic faith by an attend-
ing sister who did not think he was going to live."[11]This
tiny baby was kept in a wooden butter box and wrapped
in cotton batting.

Before long Dr. Crawford was again looking across
the seas, this time to Canada and to the tiny pioneer vil-
lage of Paisley on the Saugeen River in Bruce County. He
applied for a licence to practice medicine in the Province
of Canada on March 22, 1857. His application was
received and approved on April 1, 1857.[12] A sworn oath
taken in Toronto reads:

Fee recd £20

J.D.H.

Stephen Dennis Crawford of the Village of Paisley,
County of Bruce & Province of Canada Esquire,
Member of the Royal College of Surgeons of
England, Maketh Oath and saith that he is the person

mentioned & designated in the Diploma hereunto annexed from the said Royal College of Surgeons of England and dated the 22nd day of January A.D. 1836.

(sgd) Stephen D. Crawford

sworn before me at the
City of Toronto this first
day of April A.D. 1857

(sgd) J.D. Harrison
Judge County Court
United Counties of York and Peel

It is also recorded that doctors S. Crawford and W. Thorp were commissioned as Coroners for the United County of Huron and Bruce on November 13, 1857.[13]

With whatever hopes and dreams he had, Stephen Dennis Crawford prepared for a new life.

Two

PAISLEY

I drove to Paisley in May 1987. I wanted to see the house where the Crawford family had lived, and, if I could, I wanted to go inside. The house was still there, though it had been moved from its original site at the corner of Queen and Inkerman Streets when the new Presbyterian Church was erected in 1927. Now tucked back into a corner of the churchyard, the house stood intact, weathered and grey. I had to walk through a machine shop that was attached to the front and side of the little wooden structure to find the front door. It had been my intention to photograph the interior, but it was filled with machinery, and there was little to help one envisage how it might have looked in 1860. I did, however, photograph the exterior, then left to wander around the village.

My own great-grandparents, Hugh McDougald and Mary McNeill, had been married in Paisley on October 5, 1864 by the Reverend Bremner of Knox Church. This was, therefore, a sentimental journey for me on several accounts. Both my ancestors and Isabella beckoned.

Eric Parker my historical contact, met me at the beautiful old Town Hall, built in 1876. We spoke of Isabella, and of Dr. Crawford, and of Paisley's beginnings. A resident at Paisley, living near the old Crawford house, he alone, is responsible for ferreting out the details of 'the Crawford scandal'. We drove around the village, and I was told how it all began.

Dr. Crawford arrived in Paisley in the spring of 1857. It had only been six years prior to this, on an April evening in 1851, that Simon Orchard,[1] travelling down river on a raft with his wife and family, landed at a point of land where the Teeswater River merges with the Saugeen. The following morning, as he prepared to resume his voyage, Simon Orchard had a strange experience. His immediate surroundings were completely familiar: the lay of the land, the rich flats, the vigorous growth of forest had all appeared to him in a dream. From the few boards he had with him on his raft, and with what materials were immediately available, he constructed a temporary shanty. Within a few days, a party of men who had been surveying the Elora Road happened along and helped Simon construct a log cabin which he was able to occupy by the first of May.

On May 9, 1851 Mr. S.T. Rowe, with his family and little stock of belongings piled on two rafts made of cedar poles, arrived on the scene. Mr. Rowe, who would figure prominently in the history of Paisley, now took up his quarters on the south side of the river. He built a log shanty, and promptly opened a tavern.

In August, a Mr. John Valentine of Fergus, Ontario, selected a mill site at Mud River (Paisley). He sent two men to take possession of the property and made preparations for the erection of his mill. One of these men, David Ross, died in September, and boards were taken from the floor of Mr. Rowe's shanty to make a coffin.

In the same summer of 1851 the industrious Mr. Orchard set to work to build a bridge across the Teeswater River. He was able to put in the piers and stringers, and the following summer the span was completed. As well

Simon Orchard underbrushed a road along the left bank of the Saugeen River all the way to Southampton on the shores of Lake Huron. By 1852 other settlers were arriving and John Valentine's mill was in operation. In 1854, the year of 'The Land Sale', settlers flocked to the United County of Huron and Bruce; and, in this same year, Thomas Orchard (a brother of Simon) erected the village's first store. By 1856 a Post Office was opened, and the name *Paisley* given to the village.

At the time of the arrival of Dr. Crawford in 1857, Paisley was little more than a cluster of log houses, and most of these log houses were shanties. It was to this pioneer wilderness that Mrs. Crawford journeyed in 1858. An instrument of sale dated August 11, 1858[2] at the Registry Office in Walkerton, Ontario, shows Sydney Crawford purchased one acre of crown land (lots 17 and 18 West Regent Street South) for which she paid the sum of fifty dollars.

Mr. Parker showed me the location of this property. It was beautifully situated, just a short distance from the main street of the village, on a rise of land overlooking the Teeswater River, and not far from the house in which the Crawfords lived on Queen Street. I wonder what kind of home Sydney Scott Crawford dreamed might one day occupy that chosen spot. If, in later years, Isabella displayed an unusual strength of character, the trait must have come from her mother. Uprooted from a genteel Dublin existence, Mrs. Crawford now found herself in a rugged (albeit beautiful) backwoods Canadian hamlet.

These were the days of barter, payment for medical services was often made by delivering perhaps a cord of wood to the doctor's house, or fresh eggs or vegetables from the garden, whatever people had to offer and could spare. No ledger or account books of Dr. Crawford's were left to examine. However, ledgers of Dr. John

Hutchison[5], who practiced medicine in the town of Peterborough in the 1830s show that, although there were cash payments, provisions offered in return for services included: butter, eggs, mutton, veal, hay, fish, cheese, maple sugar, bush cranberries, whiskey and potatoes. It would seem a good table was ensured for the doctor.

One incident was recorded concerning this practice.

He [Dr. Crawford] had a very great aversion to pulling teeth, but when warmed to his work would perform even this painful duty with nerve and dispatch. On one occasion a settler went to him with an aching tooth for extraction, but the doctor advised medication and gave him a mixture to apply in the cavity. A too liberal application of the mixture was attended with serious consequences to the mouth, and again the Dr. was sought for relief. When extraction was not to be warded off any further, he inquired of the settler if he had any potatoes, and made arrangements with him to bring in a bagfull in payment for the job, and then set to work. After getting it out he told the settler to "say the word and he'd pull every tooth for the same price."[6]

This was the summer of 1858, known in Paisley as 'Starvation Year.' [7] What a time to arrive in Canada! Along with the failure of crops there was a general depression. A barrel of flour cost twenty dollars. Where was a man to find the money for such a necessity? Without money to buy and without employment available, new settlers faced a bleak future.

Is it any wonder therefore that it was an experience

which burned itself into the memories of heads of families who saw nothing but want staring them in the face, and who dreaded the moment, which appeared inevitable, when the last morsel would be gone and their children would cry for bread, with nothing to give them? To relieve the distress in a measure and ward off utter starvation, corn was brought in from the United States., which sold at a lower price than flour, and Indian meal was the stable diet of the settlement. The township councils and the provincial county council of which Mr. Valentine was that year the head took action. They adopted the plan of creating work by opening out the sidelines and concessions and giving the settlers an opportunity to earn a little money. They borrowed money to pay for this and also to buy seed wheat as well as bread to keep the people from starving, the settlers giving their notes for payment. One improvement which may be mentioned was the building of the Saugeen bridge on Goldie St., which took place in the summer of 1858.[8]

The New World must have seemed similar to the poverty that had been left behind in rural Ireland. There would not be much to offer the doctor in exchange for his services in his first year in Canada.

The Crawfords first lived in a small house on Queen Street[9], then later moved into a new home on lot 21 North, East side of Queen Street south, described in the 1861 census as being built in 1860 and evaluated at $400. This building was finished in white clapboard siding, with overlapping eaves, and boasted an upstairs nursery that ran the entire length of the house. In comparison with the other dwellings along Queen Street, it would have been quite impressive. The 1861 census lists the Crawfords as owning, in addition to the house, two horses and a carriage[10].

Although there was a little schoolhouse (Lot 11, Concession A) of flattened logs, measuring 20 x 24 feet inside, with a Miss Eliza Stewart[11] holding forth for the sum of £50 a year, the Crawford children were tutored at home by their parents. They studied French and Latin, classical literature and mythology, read Dante and Horace in translation, and were instructed in arithmetic, geography, grammar and spelling (though Isabella would continue to spell badly and use faulty grammar throughout her life). One wonders what books were available for such instruction. Certainly the Crawfords had not arrived with an extensive library, perhaps a few cherished volumes, nothing more.

It is interesting to note that as early as 1860 the more progressive and intellectual of the Paisley setters considered forming a public library. Money was contributed to purchase books, but principally volumes were donated from the libraries of local ministers, and there were more ministers than one might imagine in a pioneer community.

St. Andrew's Presbyterian Church held its first meeting in Rowe's Tavern in 1853, with an itinerant preacher, the Reverend Mr. Hutchison conducting the service. In 1856 the Reverend Kenneth McLennan was inducted as St. Andrew's minister and settled in the village. McLennan was considered 'Paisley's apostle of peace'. He was a man of the 'Auld Kirk' and said to have had a robust constitution and a readiness to adapt himself to circumstances and make the most of his surroundings. He conducted his services in Valentine's mill while he personally helped to build the little white church on the hill which opened in 1859.

Knox Presbyterian Church was organized in 1858,

possibly 1857, with the Reverend Mr. Bremner as minister in 1860. Services were held in the little log schoolhouse in the early years. The Reverend Mr. Iveson was in the Methodist pulpit at this time while the Reverend Mr. Sinclair and the Reverend Mr. McNeill were in charge of the Baptist flock.

In 1859, Bishop Cronyn, the Bishop of Huron, visited Paisley for the purpose of establishing an Anglican congregation. "The Bishop preached a telling discourse from Romans 10, 17 and during his stay was the guest of old Dr. Crawford."[12]

> Sabbath morn saw the Crawfords among the church-going villagers, the doctor dignified in his morning coat, gray plug hat and ivory-headed cane; his wife in Irish poplin and Paisley shawl and bonnet tied with brown ribbon, and the little Isabella in hoop skirt and tartan plaid with dainty frilled pantalets, beaver cloth coat and blue satin hat; the trio was followed at a respectable distance by Maggie, the faithful nurse thought to have travelled with Mrs. Crawford from Ireland with frail little Naomi by the hand.[13]

From outward appearances all was well. Legend has it that both the doctor and Mrs. Crawford were clever conversers—good raconteurs.[14] "...and elderly Paisley bodies descant even yet, upon pleasant evenings spent at the Crawfords' house, where guests were sure of a warm welcome, music and a game of whist."[15]

Among the personal treasures the Crawfords brought with them from Ireland was a harp. There were also steel engravings, Irish linens and silver for their table, Irish poplin gowns "that lasted through several refashionings," and a deep-fringed shawl that became the envy of Mrs. Crawford's friends.[16]

The number of children who arrived with Mrs. Crawford remains a puzzle. Stephen Walter, born December 25, 1856, is said to have been the twelfth child.[3] If seven of eleven children died with fever in 1855 while Dr. Crawford was in Australia[4], then five children must have accompanied their mother to Paisley. We know that Isabella, Naomi and Stephen Walter did, but what of the other two children. Did they both die while the family lived in that village? On July 2, 1927 Annie Sutherland, a granddaughter of Samuel Rowe, published an article in *The Free Press*, London, in which she told of the funeral of one of the Crawford children in Paisley.

At least this one death seems certain: "During the sorrows of the Crawfords there were kind neighbours to minister to the little dying child and sympathizing friends to bear the little casket up the long hill to the last resting place.[17]

In 1859, at the age of 45, Sydney Scott Crawford gave birth for the last time. A little girl was christened Sydney, and her name appeared on the 1861 census as Sydney R.[18]

Also in 1859, Dr. Crawford applied for the position of Elderslie Township Treasurer. It was evident the doctor was living much beyond his means and needed additional income. Causing a greater problem was his addiction to alcohol and the affect it had on his practice. A Paisley woman is reported to have said: "It is not very nice to have your baby when you didn't know if the doctor knew what he was about."[19]

What affect did all this have on the child Isabella who was not yet ten years of age? It would have been impossible to escape the tension and the heartache inevitable in such a household. Fortunately for her, she could escape through her keen observation and her imagination.

On the verges of the pioneer village she would see trees felled, fields cleared and ploughed, and crops sown. She would store in her memory, man's struggle with the land, and later these vivid impressions would record themselves in the lines of *Malcolm's Katie*:

> ...I heard him tell
> How the first field upon his farm was ploughed.
> He and his brother Reuben, stalwart lads,
> Yoked themselves, side by side, to the new plough;
> Their weaker father, in the grey of life—
> But rather the wan age of poverty
> Than many winters—in large, gnarled hands
> The plunging handles held; with mighty strains
> They drew the ripping beak through knotted sod,
> Thro' tortuous lanes of blackened, smoking stumps,
> And past great flaming brush-heaps, sending out
> Fierce summers, beating on their swollen brows.
>
> Malcolm's Katie Part I
> lines 70 - 72

If there were bad times, there were good times as well. *Antrim* tells us that Isabella often travelled with her father to the Indian camps in the Saugeen area:

> ...she was their Nenemoosha (sweetheart): for her they wove their prettiest baskets and beaded moccasins while she watched them and she carried away with her, too, the beaded bag of many gay colours... Years after when the Ojibways had all settled together at Chippewa, they came regularly to Paisley selling their woven mats, baskets of sweet hay...and more than once asked at the white house on the corner for the "Medicine Man" and the young girl.[20]

She was remembered by an old pioneer as "a fair, frail girl, with great, blue, dreamy eyes."[21] Catherine Crawford Humphrey, great granddaughter of Dr. Crawford, believes that it was here in Paisley that Isabella began to write verse and compose fairy tales.

On March 18, 1861 the Regent Street and the Queen Street properties owned by the Crawford's were mortgaged for five hundred dollars to Thomas Brighty of Southampton. Shortly after this, Dr. Crawford and his family left the village of Paisley.

> Early in 1861 Dr. Hill came to share with him (Crawford) the honour of keeping the settlement in good health, and in September of the same year Dr. McLaren. When Dr. McLaren came to Paisley, Dr. Crawford had just left.[22]

In 1865 the *Paisley Advocate* began publishing. In this newspaper, township council meetings were given some prominence. Eric Parker, through his research on the town, unearthed a scandal involving Dr. Crawford.

In the years 1858 and 1859 Thomas Orchard was Treasurer of the Township of Elderslie. At the close of the latter year he requested an increase in salary, threatening to resign if he did not receive this increase. Council accepted his resignation and advertised for another treasurer. Dr. Crawford, the sole applicant, was appointed to the office; and proposed as his sureties, Messrs. F.O. Lynch Staunton, Enoch C. Dowling and Robert Gilmour. These gentlemen were accepted as such, and bonds duly executed. When Dr. Crawford left Paisley and five hundred dollars was discovered missing from the township accounts, an investigative committee was formed by the township council.

A writ was issued December 15, 1863: ."in the suit of the Corporation of the Township of Elderslie against Stephen Crawford, F.H. Lynch Staunton, Enoch C. Dowling and Robert Gilmour." [23]

The wealthiest bondsman was Enoch C. Dowling. All his properties (which were considerable) were seized to satisfy the judgment in the Crawford case. These were sold by the sheriff to a Goderich lawyer, Lewis A. Moore for two hundred and twenty-five dollars. The financially-ruined Enoch C. Dowling committed suicide, leaving behind him a pregnant widow.[24]

On December 27, 1865 the Crawford properties (3 parcels) were acquired by Robert Dick from Thomas Brighty through power of sale.

Further scandal came to light. In 1866, a Mr. W.C. Bruce was elected Deputy Reeve. He was accused of having whiskey brought to the nomination meeting, of being involved in a road-grant scheme involving fraud, and of receiving money from Dr. Crawford in 1860 and 1861 which he knew to be township funds. This last accusation was refuted by a Mr. Featherstonehaugh: "In a conversation held some years since with Dr. Crawford, he told me that he was wrongfully accused of having paid township money to you [W.C. Bruce] and that the money which he had paid you was the proceeds of a mortgage, and I think also, as well as my memory serves, that he had some of it from the old country."[25]

Why did Dr. Crawford owe W.C. Bruce money? What are we to believe? If nothing else, it was all a tragic mess. Gone were the hopes and dreams for a new beginning in Upper Canada. The Crawford family disappeared from Bruce County in disgrace.

Wrong →
1st settlers were
John + Margaret
Nelson in 1819
it was called
Nelson Falls.
Then Herriot Fall
Then Lakefield

Three

LAKEFIELD

The village of Lakefield had its beginnings in 1831 when Col. Samuel Strickland arrived from England and started his "Farm School" for gentlemen agriculturists. Back in 'the old country' members of his family were famed for their literary achievements. Samuel added to the family reputation with his book *Twenty-seven Years in Canada West, 1853*.

In 1832 Samuel was joined in Lakefield by his sister, Catherine Parr Traill, and her husband, Lieutenant Thomas Traill. Another sister, Susanna, and her husband, John Dunbar Moodie, also emigrated to Lakefield in 1834. It was because of the Strickland family settlement that, in later years, the area would become known as "the cradle of Canadian literature."[1]

The village was located in the heart of the Kawartha Lakes where Lake Katchewanooka meets the Otonabee River. Many settlers were attracted to the beautiful region, among them 'people of culture'. As Katherine Hale snobbishly expressed, "There were several old English families living in or near the village and hence congenial society."[2] Through a strange twist of fate and the benevolence of Robert Strickland, son of Col. Strickland, the Crawford family found themselves living in an elegant home in Lakefield,[3] or North Douro as it was then known.

In the summer of 1864 my brother and I travelling for the Canada Company throughout Eastern Canada, happened to put up for the night at a village hotel, north of Kingston.

There we met Dr. Crawford, at that time a man of nearly sixty years of age, his wife, a son and two daughters. The eldest of these daughters afterwards turned out to be that great poetess of Canada, Isabella Valancy Crawford.

They seemed to be very poorly off and we felt really sorry for them out here in Canada amidst such unsuitable surroundings. My brother, knowing that there was no resident physician in the village of Lakefield, made to them the following offer, 'That they move to Lakefield and make use of his home during the months he would be away from the village'.

His offer was accepted and presently Dr. Crawford and family came to the village and he took up practice being the first resident practitioner that Lakefield acquired."[4]

The date of this encounter, 1864, is incorrect. However, such an error is understandable when we realize sixty years had passed since that chance meeting and the writing of the account by Frank Dobbin.

When did the Crawfords arrive in Lakefield? Recently I was made aware of a letter written by Catherine Parr Traill, dated October 27, supposedly in 1861.

Westove

My Dearest Friend—
...Previous to her illness I was much away from her with Percy's wife who was confined on the 12th of

the month with a fine little girl. Dr. Crawford was her attendant and Mrs. Shairpe and myself assistants.[5]

If this letter was indeed written in 1861, then Dr. Crawford was in Lakefield shortly after leaving Paisley. We do know definitely, however, that in the autumn of 1862 Dr. Crawford was making purchases at Sherin's Store:

#157 Dr. Crawford per self
Thursday 6th November 1862
5 scanes worsted yarn   .14   .70
100 cwt bran   2.50

#157 Dr. Crawford per self
Saturday 6th December 1862
1 turkey   .50
2 1/2 yards flanal   1.38
1 tie   .09

#157 Dr. Crawford per self
Monday 22nd December 1862
10 yds organzy   3.79
1 lb soda crackers   .13
2 1.2 yds lining   .45 [6]

I found myself pleased to see that a few weeks before Christmas, Isabella's father purchased a turkey, and that on December 22, he chose to buy silk and lining. The Crawfords were now living in Reydon Hall, the beautiful home of Robert Strickland, a home as lovely today as it was then.

Named for the Strickland home in Suffolk, England, Reydon Hall represented gracious living of the time. A personal wander through the home revealed to the left the drawing room off the main entrance, with the dining room to the right. Both rooms were spacious and airy with high ceilings and a fireplace. Behind the drawing room was the library containing a desk that once belonged to Col. Samuel Strickland. The kitchen was at the rear with sheds beyond. From the wide reception hall a balustered staircase led to the second floor. Upstairs the bedrooms were equally inviting and one could see, through the wavy antique glass of the original window-panes, the carefully tended lawns that sloped to the water's edge.

I like to think that Dr. Crawford came home that week before Christmas in 1862 and carefully stored the turkey out of harm's way in some cold backshed where it would 'keep' until the festive day. Perhaps he presented his wife with the silk organza so she might have a gown worthy of her surroundings.

Isabella would have her twelfth birthday that Christmas and Stephen Walter his sixth. Emma Naomi, or Naomi as she was called by her family, was eight years old. In the Dobbin's account of the Crawford-Strickland meeting north of Kingston: "...There we met Dr. Crawford, at that time a man of nearly sixty years of age, his wife, a son and two daughters" no reference was made to the child Sydney R., born in Paisley in 1859 and listed in the 1861 census. It is possible that while the Strickland brothers discussed the doctor's proposed future in Lakefield, the little Sydney was asleep in her bed, watched-over and tended-to by some young maid servant at the Inn.

In the cemetery records of Christ Church, North Douro, a burial is recorded:

Rebecca Anne Crawford, Age 5, cause of death Scarlet Fever, buried in Lakefield Churchyard, March

22nd, 1864. Vincent Clementi officiating.[7]

Was this the child Sydney R.? Did the "R" stand for Rebecca? Sydney R. would have been five years old, the date would substantiate such speculation. There is another reason to believe the child born to Mrs. Crawford in 1859 was with them in Lakefield:

>...Isabella was the oldest child.... There was a boy Steven and two other girls. They lost these two girls while living here (Lakefield) or in Peterborough where they lived after they left Lakefield.[8]

Apart from these records, no further reference to this youngest child has been found.

In Lakefield, as elsewhere in those times, if accepted by local middle-class society, one could enjoy a variety of pleasant gatherings and outings. There were dinner parties often followed by an evening of charades, church functions, pigeon shoots, regattas on the lake in summer, picnics and canoeing; and in winter, ice skating on Buckley Lake. Isabella was invited to participate. Hopes were resurrected, the Crawfords were to have another chance in society. "Sometimes Isabella would decline to go to the merrymakings of the young people, but when she did attend," recalls a Lakefield contemporary, "she became the life of the party, electrifying us with her flashes of wit and repartee."[9]

If there was ever a happy time in the life of Isabella Valancy Crawford, it is likely to have been those early Lakefield years.

> There ne'er was born out of the yellow east
> So fresh, so fair, so sweet a morn as this.

The dear earth decked herself as for a feast;
And, as for me, I trembled with my bliss.

Said the Daisy
lines 1-4

In October 1863 the Reverend Vincent Clementi,
who had emigrated from England in 1855, was appoint-
ed Rector of Christ Church. He was the son of Muzio
Clementi, a renowned Italian composer, musician, and
father of the pianoforte. His arrival in Lakefield added
another dimension to Isabella's life. It is thought that he
instructed her in music and taught her to play the piano
which, it is said, she did with competence:

> Her passion for music was almost as great as her love
> for books and poetry. She studied the piano and
> played very well indeed, collecting a good deal of
> music.[10]

Dr. Crawford involved himself in the affairs of the
community. When Christ Church (where Isabella is
believed to have received her confirmation) became too
small for a growing congregation, a building committee
for a new church was formed. The doctor served on this
committee to oversee the building of St. John the Baptist
Church.

Dr. Crawford's name does not appear (in the list of
those present at Vestry meetings) until March, 1864
and it was last recorded on October 9, 1866. It had
been proposed that a new church be built, and at the
vestry meeting of 1864, Doctor Crawford was
among those elected to the building committee.
During the period of planning and construction and
until the completion of the church, five Vestry meet-
ings and seven meetings of the building committee

were held. According to the records, Doctor Crawford missed only one Vestry and one committee meeting. The last meeting to record his name was held "to arrange about sittings in the new church." This meeting was also attended by a Mrs. Crawford, I presume his wife."[11]

Fortunately for us the Strickland sisters were eager correspondents, many of their letters have been preserved. Through some of these letters we are allowed glimpses into the Crawford lives and Dr. Crawford's ministering:

...Mrs. Percy has a fine son, but Alice is ill with Scarlet Fever and Susan has been in great distress, and of course Percy most anxious, he was here yesterday and says she is better, he came for currant jelly to make a drink for the sweet lamb. Dr. Crawford says that half the deaths are caused by too much medicine at first. He brought little Gill through who was very bad indeed.

and

..Dr. C says nothing is worse for a young child than mothers letting them sit overlong in a chair or Po— as it forces down these parts and weakens the body, so dear child take heed about your boy.[12]

As was the custom among Victorian ladies, young and old, journals were kept and events of the day faithfully recorded. Catherine Parr Traill made these notations:

November 20th, 1863

After a fortnight of wet sunless weather, a real Indian

summer day—Night frost morning misty—the sun
rose red through the fog—A day of surpassing love-
liness soft warm balmy...Miss Crawford and Miss
Valentine called for a few minutes.[13]

There was not a Valentine family living in the area. It
may have been a daughter of John Valentine, a friend of
Paisley days.

April 15th, 1864

On the 5th received a summons to go to Caroline's,
my nephew Robts wife, she being taken very ill and
her nurse not having come yet to her—A most severe
and dangerous labour—the infant was born before
the doctor came into the room—but a melancholy
disease in the spine was discovered in the newborn
babe—the beauty of the child's face and bust had
made me congratulate the mother to cheer her suf-
fering condition—but it was indeed shouts before
victory and the shouts proved greater than I was able
to endure especially as I had to conceal my distress of
mind as the poor mother seemed in so alarming a
state that we feared her death momentarily—God in
his goodness spared the mother and took the babe
after several days of wasting, the spirit of the young
child returned to God who gave it—it was bap-
tized—Ethel—About five o'clock I became very ill—
a dreadful headache burning and swelling of my face
with throbbing pain—This increased almost to
agony—I tried to make tea for Drs. McNabb and
Crawford but was seized with some sort of fit and
finally carried to my brother's house where I
swooned several times. For many days I was confined
to my bed in great weakness of body suffering from

neuralgia of the heart and other maladies. On the first week in May I was able to return home.[14]

July 7th 1865

The doctor Crawford at nine o'clock p.m. gave into my arms a little grandson a fair delicate babe—whom may God bless and preserve.[15]

In this same year, Catherine Parr Traill's sister, Susanna Moodie, described the village of Lakefield as it appeared to her:

July 10, 1865

...How rapidly the face of this country changes. I left the woods of North Douro, 26 years ago. Only three houses all composed of logs and of the smallest dimensions were to be found within three miles of us. Now, my brother, who may be termed the Father and founder of the village of Lakefield, has a handsome commodious house and a beautiful garden which would amply satisfy the taste of any gentleman of moderate fortune, four of his five lads are married and settled near him. A neat village consisting of pretty, well built houses, has sprung up like magic, where the lovely falls once foamed and thundered in the heart of the forest. The hand of industry has curbed the wild torrent and made it subservient to the wants of men. The stumps are almost all gone, and tasteful gardens full of bright flowers meet the eye in every direction. The place has already four churches, and they are busy building a very handsome new Episcopal Church. The old one raised 12 years ago, is not half large enough to contain its worshippers. My Uncle's son Walter is the architect, a young man of such taste and talent. To keep even, the balance of good and evil, there are as many taverns as churches. A post office, a daily stage to and from Peterboro, a fine town, now 10 miles distant—three stores [in Lakefield] a bakery, 2 large saw mills and many pretty villas belonging to the gentlemen settlers. I was charmed by the lovely scenery, with the air of comfort and general improvement that pervades the place. The people are kind and friendly. And why? No lawyer has as yet shewed the cloven foot among them. And the hilly country is so healthy that the one doctor barely ekes out a living.[16]

The one doctor referred to is, of course, Dr. Crawford. And now the tides of fortune were to turn once more. Dr. Crawford's practice proved no more successful in Lakefield than it had in Paisley. As well his reputation suffered from his excessive drinking: "Mother, who only met them on a visit to Lakefield, and so only knew them from hearsay, thinks Dr. C. took too much milk punch."[17]
There was a story of a Mr. Squire who accidentally shot himself in the leg. Dr. Crawford amputated the leg and apparently 'bungled' the job, so that it was necessary to amputate still more of the limb. Consequently Mr. Squire died.[18] Residents of the village were losing confidence in Dr. Crawford's abilities, and were seeking other medical opinions. This was apparent as early as 1864.

On Monday morning, September 5th, a happy party started for the Lakes in North Douro. It consisted of William and Louise Stewart, their little son Tom and Robert McNabb. All went prosperously, and on the 7th they set out in two canoes for another day of pleasure. But alas, how uncertain are all our enjoyments!

"Thornberry", #55 and 53 Malborough Road, Dublin. Home of the Crawfords. *Elizabeth Galvin, December 1989*

The Crawford Home in Paisley, Ontario, corner of Queen and Inkerman Streets. *Elizabeth Galvin*

Lakefield-Reydon Hall, the Robert Strickland home in Lakefield, Ontario, where the Crawfords lived 1862-63. *Elizabeth Galvin*

House south-west corner of George and Edinburgh Streets, Peterborough, Ontario where Dr. Crawford died in 1875. *Elizabeth Galvin*

Ryan's Terrace, Market Square, Peterborough, Ontario. *Courtesy Peterborough Centennial Museum*

57 John Street, Toronto, Ontario, where the poet died February 12, 1887. *Courtesy Metro Toronto Library*

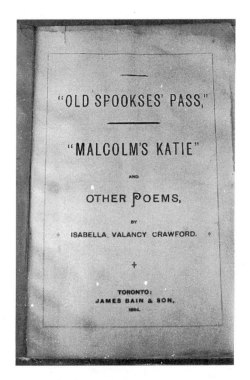

Title page, "Old Spookses' Pass Malcolm's Katie and Other Poems", 1884 first edition. *Courtesy Peterborough Public Library*

Isabella Valancy Crawford and facsimile of her poem "Faith, Hope and Charity", *Canadian Singers and their Songs.* Toronto: William Briggs, 1902. *Courtesy Peterborough Public Library*

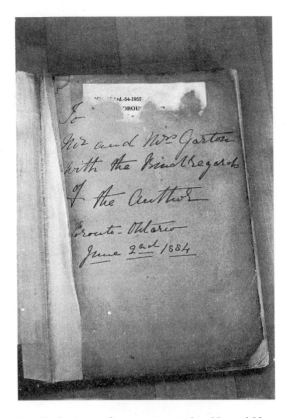

Inscribed volume of poetry presented to Mr. and Mrs.
Garton. *Courtesy Peterborough Public Library*

"Old Spookses' Pass", *Courtesy Peterborough Public
Library*

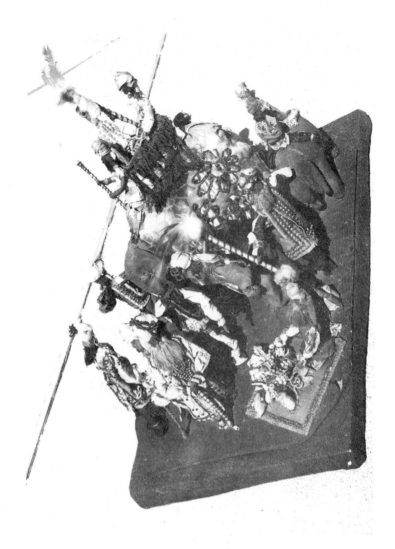

Embroidered sculpture *Indian Pageant.* Photographed with permission
of the Peterborough Centennial Museum.. *Courtesy of The Roy Studio,
Peterborough, Ontario*

An older Isabella Valancy
Crawford from article by
"Jeanette", *Peterborough
Examiner*, 20 March, 1934
*Courtesy Martha Kidd,
Elizabeth Farquharson*

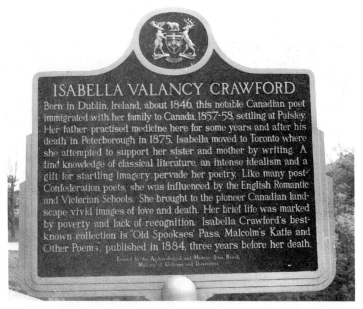

ISABELLA VALANCY CRAWFORD

Born in Dublin, Ireland, about 1846, this notable Canadian poet
immigrated with her family to Canada, 1857-58, settling at Paisley.
Her father practised medicine here for some years and after his
death in Peterborough in 1875, Isabella moved to Toronto where
she attempted to support her sister and mother by writing. A
fine knowledge of classical literature, an intense idealism and a
gift for startling imagery pervade her poetry. Like many post-
Confederation poets, she was influenced by the English Romantic
and Victorian Schools. She brought to the pioneer Canadian land-
scape vivid images of love and death. Her brief life was marked
by poverty and lack of recognition. Isabella Crawford's best-
known collection is 'Old Spookses' Pass, Malcolm's Katie and
Other Poems', published in 1884, three years before her death.

Erected by the Archaeological and Historic Sites Board,
Ministry of Colleges and Universities

This plaque in Paisley, Ontario was unveiled by the Archaeological and
Museum Sites Board October 5, 1974.

September 9th, 1983. Senator Andrew Thompson and Alderman Roy Wood unveil Historic Sites and Monuments Board of Canada plaque in Scott's Plains Park, Peterborough, Ontario. *Courtesy Historic Sites and Monuments of Canada*

Dr. Patricia Fleming unveiling the Toronto Historical Board plaque May 21, 1992. Looking on: Mr. William Crawford, (great-nephew of Isabella), Councillor Liz Amer, Toronto City Council, Mrs. Anne Sutherland-Brooks, Miss Doris Tucker, Women's Canadian Historical Society. *Toronto Historical Board*

Christ Church, Lakefield, where Isabella Valancy Crawford was confirmed. *Elizabeth Galvin*

St. John's Anglican Church, Hunter Street, Peterborough. *Elizabeth Galvin*

Gail Corbett, President of the Peterborough Branch, Canadian Authors'
Association, places a white rose on the Crawford grave on the occasion
of the 100th anniversary of the poet's burial in Little Lake Cemetery
March 4, 1987. *Elizabeth Galvin*

Inscription on Crawford's stone. *Elizabeth Galvin*

Our dearest William, in taking his gun to shoot at a crane, by some means wounded his arm near the elbow. At once they bound it up tightly. Of course they turned homeward, and dear William tried to help paddle but his arm bled so profusely that he could not continue and he directed Robert to tighten the bandage by twisting it with a stick, but Robert became too nervous to do so. Mr. Fuller joined them afterwards and helped them to Young's Point; he also tried to tighten the bandage, but all in vain. Poor William grew weaker till they reached Lakefield. When I heard the sad news of the accident I went to the village, and then met Eliza McNabb, and we went together to the lake shore to wait for the boats to come in, which they did about six or half-past six o'clock. Poor William seemed very much exhausted, so I did not speak to him then. The first time I spoke to him was when he was laid on the verandah at Dr. Crawford's, still in the canoe...As soon as he was laid on a bed I left him, intending to return for the night.

When I returned, between nine and ten o'clock I found Dr. McNabb (who had been sent for) had arrived. I believe from the first Dr. McNabb had no hopes. And Dr. Burnham, who arrived about three in the morning, confirmed the sad truth.[19]

Of course it would be appropriate to call in other doctors for a consultation in such grave circumstances, yet one cannot help feeling Dr. Crawford's ministerings may have been considered less than adequate.

The Collector's Rolls for the Township of Douro show that in 1863 Dr. Crawford was a householder on West Regent Street, Lot 6, with 1/4 acre. In 1864, these same Rolls have Dr. Crawford living west of Strickland Street, Lot 1, with 1/3 acre, and 2 dogs (did someone

give the doctor two puppies in exchange for medical ser-
vices?) The Collector's Rolls also show that Dr. Crawford
served in the Reserve Militia in 1864.

> They [the Crawfords] afterwards lived in a little
> house where Mother remembers going with Aunt
> Kate and Grandmother to take tea with them...
> Isabella was the oldest child—at the time about sev-
> enteen years old (Mother can't remember the date)
> very pretty, medium complexion, very pretty hair,
> which she did in the same style as Empress Eugenie
> of France—rolled back from the face. Mother does-
> n't think she had written anything up to that time
> but she spoke of writing a book which she was going
> to call "Lavender and Old Lace." There was to be an
> old lady in it dressed in velvet with lavender trim-
> mings and old lace and ribbons in cap etc. ...They
> were proud and not at all friendly and although poor
> resented any kindness—suspecting patronage where
> people meant to be kind and friendly as was the way
> in those early days... It was when they were living in
> Peterborough that Doctor Crawford died. They
> became so poor that they almost starved, but so
> painfully proud that their nearest neighbours did not
> realize the extent of their poverty.[20]

Isabella was indeed writing during these Lakefield
years. Her signature, *Isabella Valancy*, appeared at the end
of a fairy tale, "*The Waterlily*", found in manuscript form,
with the address North Douro [Lakefield] written on the
back of the last page.[21]

The world was changing rapidly around her.
However, if life was difficult for Isabella, there were oth-
ers whose sufferings were far greater. She heard tales of
families torn apart by the conflicts of the American Civil

War. She railed at the injustice of society, but she accepted its challenge. As so often happens, adversity strengthened her purpose and her purpose was to write. Aware of the gossip concerning her father, Isabella withdrew more and more from the social life of the village. Her clothes were shabby, she could not entertain in kind. Never mind, she did not need that kind of association. With her fertile imagination, she would never know boredom. She fictionalized lives and situations, manipulated them and found a certain measure of happiness in her creativity.

Queen Victoria signed the British North America Act on March 2, 1867. It was proclaimed that as of noon on July 1, 1867, the four provinces of Ontario, Quebec, Nova Scotia and New Brunswick would form in Confederation, the Dominion of Canada. In the enlightened Crawford household this significant event would have been discussed.

The times have won a change. Nature no more
Lords it alone and binds the lonely land
A serf to tongueless solitudes; but Nature's self
Is led, glad captive, in light fetters rich
As music-sounding silver can adorn;
And man has forged them, and our silent God
Behind his flaming worlds smiles on the deed.
"Man hath dominion"—words of primal might,
"Man hath dominion"—thus the words of God.
                              Canada to England
                              lines 19-27

Isabella heard much talk of railroads, and the one that would be built to stretch 'from sea to sea'. She heard of growing commerce and what all this would mean to places such as Lakefield and Peterborough.

Then came smooth-coated men with eager eyes
And talked of steamers on the cliff-bound lakes,
And iron tracks across the prairie lands,
And mills to crush the quartz of wealthy hills,
And mills to saw the great wide-armed trees,
And mills to grind the singing stream of grain.
And with such busy clamour mingled still
The throbbing music of the bold, bright Axe—
The steel tongue of the present; and the wail
Of falling forests—voices of the past.

Malcolm's Katie Part II
lines 233-241

It has been suggested that *Old Spookses' Pass* was written during the Lakefield years. This seems unlikely, as Isabella was still in her teens and lacked the maturity to produce such a work. However the substance of the story of *Malcolm's Katie* was all around her. Not far away, in Smith Township, the Mississaugas had been located at the Curve Lake Indian Reservation of Mud Lake (Chemong). The Mississaugas hunted and fished in the area. Isabella watched these native people as she had those of Bruce County, and her imagination was fuelled. Some of her most beautiful poetry concerns native myth and legend:

For love is the breath of the soul set free;
So I cross the river that darkly rolls,
That my spirit may whisper soft to thee
Of thine who wait in the "Camp of Souls."
When the bright day laughs, or the wan night grieves,
Comes the dusky plumes of red "Singing Leaves."

The Camp of Souls
lines 67-72

As well, all aspects of the lumbering industry were close at hand for Isabella to absorb in detail:

> It was interesting to watch the cribs of square timber as they raced the rapids from Lakefield and over the number of slides on the dams. How they plunged into the foaming billows below, frequently sousing the men to the neck as they held onto the rope which alone kept them from a death struggle in the angry waters. One year, five poor fellows were the victims of a broken slide. People went to Dickson Dam in hundreds to watch the cribs make their plunge. Frequently the shantymen brought down the shanty pig on the crib and his pigship may have enjoyed the quick trip from Lakefield, but I never learned how he enjoyed the sousing he got at every dam.
>
> The river drivers on reaching Peterborough refreshed themselves and then rode back to Lakefield, chanting merry French songs, again to repeat their dangerous trip. From Peterborough the cribs went their way down the river through Rice Lake and the Trent River, rafting at Trenton and then in great cribs passed down the St. Lawrence to Quebec.[22]

And so Isabella observed all that was about her, mulling over and storing in her mind, the every-day events of a country emerging from the wilderness—the 'stuff' of her narrative poems.

Once again, through the correspondence of Catherine Parr Traill, we catch a glimpse of the Crawfords. We also learn that Kate Traill, thought to have been a friend of Isabella's was indeed just that:

My own dear Katie—

...I went yesterday to the dear old house and felt for all its loneliness a feeling of joy at being within its deserted but free walls—I lighted a good fire and staid there till late in the afternoon. I had to get some of the MS and paper for copying—Dear Sister had got me a slice of bread - and butter and a morsel of mince pie to eat—so that I did not starve while at home.

I was driven there but had to walk back—I am very lame and suffering acute pain in the knee and a sharp return of the old lumbago and sciatica so that by the time I got to Casements I was obliged to beg for a stick—My next halt was made at Dr. Crawfords, when there I felt too weary to get on further and remained for nearly an hour and Isabella would put on her cloak and hat to help me home crawling along. Mrs. Jades, Fanny, Emma and Julia overtook us and I was very glad of the lift to the gate I assure you.

The Dr. has been alarmingly ill so that it was believed he was dying but is now better again—Poor Isabella was very low, she regretted your absence she said very much and seemed to wish to write to you. I told her that I would enclose a note in this, but I do not know if she will have it ready.[23]

The J.C. Connor's *County of Peterborough Directory* for 1870 and 1871 has Stephen Crawford M.D. listed as a tenant residing in Smith Township, Concession 8, part lot 27. This information is misleading as the Crawford family were known to be in Peterborough in 1870. There is, however, among the Crawford manuscripts, an exercise book that belonged to Stephen Walter. In it he has written: "Make your letters all the same size. March 4, 1869, Lakefield, Smithtown."[24] This would indicate they were living on the Smith Township side of the river in the village of Lakefield. There had been three moves since the Crawfords first took up residence in Lakefield. We would be happy to think they were bettering themselves—unfortunately, this was not so.

Dr. Alexander Bell arrived in the village of Lakefield in 1864. In an article *The Pioneer Doctors*[25] written by Dr. Raymore Scott, Bell is referred to as the village's first resident doctor. Bell also served as Village Clerk in 1866. With the growing popularity of this new physician, the demand for Dr. Crawford's services lessened.

For some years Dr. Crawford's brother, John Irwin Crawford, a staff surgeon in the Royal Navy, had been sending the family a quarterly stipend. However, in 1869, he is reported to have lost his sight,[26] and on June 17, 1869 was superannuated from the Royal Navy, with a pension of £380 per annum.[27] The allowance ceased. If the family were to survive financially, something had to be done immediately to increase Dr. Crawford's practice.

On October 16, 1869 Dr. S.D. Crawford registered a change of address with the College of Physicians and Surgeons in Toronto.[28]

On February 17, 1870 an advertisement appeared in the *Peterborough Examiner*.

S.D. Crawford, M.D. C.M.
Member of the Royal College of Surgeons, England
Licentiate Government Medical Board
Late Resident Coombe Lying-In Hospital, Dublin
Ryan's Building, Market Square, Peterboro

Four

PETERBOROUGH

That old square which harbored the first of everything—the first Government house, the first store, the first saloon, the first circus and theatre and murder and hanging and suicide—in the municipal life of what was at first called "The Plains" by the Indians, and is now the Peterborough we know, that old square saw also the residence of the first poet.[1]

D r. Crawford moved with his family into a terrace row of houses at the corner of Water and Charlotte Streets, and it was there that he set up his medical practice. Ryan's terrace was in the center of the town's commercial district and considered a most respectable address. Other professional men had offices in this same location, among them, Dr. Thomas W. Poole.[2] Although the front windows of their home overlooked the busy market square, the Otonabee River flowed beneath the rear windows.

The town of Peterborough, located on the shores of the Otonabee River, was almost one hundred miles northeast of Toronto. In the days of its earliest settlement, it was relatively easy to reach from Lake Ontario. A trek overland from Coburg to Rice Lake led to travel by scow across the lake and up the river to what was first known as Scott's Plains. By 1820 Adam Scott had built a dam on a site where Jackson Creek enters the river. Within a short time he was operating a saw and gristmill, as well as making whiskey for sale. In 1825 the Honourable Peter Robinson was responsible for bringing more than two thousand Irish immigrants to the area and, in his honour, the name of Scott's Plains was changed to Peterborough.

Fifty years brought many changes. By the time the Crawfords arrived in town there were numerous well-established businesses, beautiful churches and stately homes. The population in 1871 was 4,611 and, when the boundaries were extended in 1872, the number of residents approached 7,000. There were sawmills, lumber mills and gristmills. There were wagon factories, tanning factories and woolen mills. There were schools and hotels, banks and insurance companies, and nearby, all manner of shops. Important to Isabella was the establishment of the Mechanic's Institute lending library in 1868, with its reading room and membership of 139.

Coinciding with the arrival of the Crawford family in Peterborough was one of the worst snow storms in history. Snow started falling on March 13, 1870 and continued intermittently until the 19th. Business was suspended and funerals postponed. Communication with the outside world was by telegraph and people could only make their way about on snowshoes. Frank Dobbin tells us in *Our Old Home Town*[3] that in cleaning off the sidewalks on George Street, from Brock to King Street, a distance of four blocks, the snow was piled so high that only the bottom of the second storey windows could be seen. At the corner of George and Simcoe Streets the snow barricade was eleven feet high. Then the warm weather of April created a thaw. The flooding was so extensive that all the dams along the river gave way. The Otonabee became a raging torrent and Little Lake spilled over, making streets south of Sherbrooke Street impassable. Funerals that reached Little Lake Cemetery did so by using punts and skiffs.

And there in Ryan's Terrace, amidst such turmoil, Isabella Valancy Crawford settled in to write.

Dr. Crawford ought to have been able to establish a medical practice in the Peterborough of that time, for among the 7,000 population were many professional and business men whose financial success was evident. The Crawfords should have enjoyed a pleasant social life as there were numerous people of refined cultural tastes. For the doctor, this was a last-ditch effort. Had he been able to overcome his alcoholism, all might have gone well. It was not to be.

The family became members of St. John's Anglican Church on Hunter Street and for two years rented pew No. 31.[4] In the beginning, ladies of the congregation 'called' at the Crawford residence, only to be told that Mrs. Crawford was not receiving guests. Visitors were unwelcome, one never knew how the doctor 'might be', and often there was not a fire in the parlour.[5] Mrs. Crawford and her daughters were much too proud to expose their poor household. All else could be and would be endured, but they would not suffer pity.

And so the girl who had been described in early Lakefield days as being 'the life of the party' further withdrew into her shell.

> She was never quite at home in town. Her manner was slightly eccentric, as a result, perhaps, of humiliating poverty, or of the fact she had little in common with the people that she met; she was thoughtful, retiring and studious, and there is little doubt that the 'eccentricity' ascribed to her was due to the con-

trast between the quiet thoughtfulness of this girl and the frivolity and worldliness of others of her age. A lady, recently deceased, Mrs. J.C. Smith, remembered that she and her little companions used to call after the poet on the street "Isabella Valancy Crawford", not in derision, nor yet in admiration, but "because she could write poetry and had a queer name." This lady recalled also, that her mother, the late Mrs. J.D. Hall, admired Miss Crawford's poetry, and used to read it to her children.[6]

According to the Peterborough Directory, Assessment Roll of the Town, during the years 1870-1874, the Crawford family resided at 324 Water Street.[7] It is interesting and amusing to note that, in this directory, the age of Dr. Crawford is given as 50 in 1870, as 57 in 1871, and as 60 in 1873. This unreliable and unsatisfactory source also mentions that five people were in residence in 1870, and only four in 1871. It is conceivable that Stephen Walter left home at this early date to seek his fortune in the northern District of Algoma. He would have been a mere boy of fifteen, but there was no hope of a university education, and land could be purchased more cheaply in the north. However, in the years 1873 and 1874, once again, according to the records, there were five people living at 324 Water Street.

Isabella Valancy Crawford appears as a sensitive girl, a young woman now in her early twenties who had been forced to endure poverty and humiliation with little hope of changing her lot in life. Little hope, that is, unless through her writing she could earn money, a lot of money. Isabella experienced desperation. She must write and she must sell what she wrote.

On December 24, 1873 Isabella published her first poem "The Vesper Star" in *The Mail*, a Toronto newspaper.

During the next seventeen months, ten other poems were also published in that paper.[8]

That same year, Isabella entered her story, *Winona, the Indian Queen*,[9] in a competition. She was awarded a prize of $600. What riches! A cheque for $100 arrived and then came the devastating news that the corporation giving the prize had failed and that no further money would be forthcoming.

Katherine Hale tells us, "Two pathetic incidents stand out in this period. The delicate Emma Naomi, the younger sister, was always busy with beautiful and intricate designs in embroidery. On one piece she had worked for a year, and sent it, in hopes of a sale or a prize, to the Centennial Exhibition at Philadelphia. It was lost in the mails."[10] The other incident to which Hale refers is, of course, Isabella's heartbreaking loss of the prize money.

Catherine Crawford Humphrey writes: "Not only did Naomi lose her beautiful bedspread in the mails, but also a hand-done lace tablecloth which she sent to Tiffany's in New York in the hope of selling it."[11]

Isabella submitted her stories to every available market. On November 6, 1874 "Moloch" appeared in *The Mail*. Printed with the poem were these credits: Isabella Valancy Crawford, also the author of "Wrecked", "Hate", "Winona", "Windale's Souvenir" etc.[12]

In New York city at this time lived a man by the name of Frank Leslie. He was responsible for numerous publications, among them, the *Popular Monthly*. Inexpensive yet attractive, this publication printed stories by some of the best known writers of the time. Isabella's stories were accepted. This recognition became her lifeline.

In 1875 Dr. Crawford found it necessary to give up his Market Square location and move to a house which still stands on the south-west corner of George and Edinburgh Streets. Contrary to what has been written, this new location was in an attractive residential neighbourhood, in a large house owned by Robert Johnson. It was here, at this address, that on July 3, 1875 Dr. Stephen Dennis Crawford suffered a fatal heart attack.

Following the death of Dr. Crawford, the financial responsibility fell heavily on Isabella's shoulders. The remaining family moved into a 'little roughcast cottage hidden by lilacs' on Brock Street. There is a difference of opinion as to where this house was located. Some believe it to have been the recently demolished cottage at 113 Brock Street. However, it is generally agreed that the little house was located across the road from the old Brock Street arena: "This house was the place opposite the Brock Street rink which was torn down last summer (1933) to make way for the new Orange Hall."[13]

On January 20, 1876, further tragedy struck. Isabella's beloved younger sister, Naomi, died of consumption. She too is buried in Peterborough's Little Lake Cemetery. At the time of her death, the family was living in a small house on Aylmer Street, somewhere between McDonnel and London Streets. Stephen Walter came home, and with his friend, William C. Nicholls, (magistrate and first coroner of the village of Lakefield) went to the cemetery on a bitterly cold January morning to purchase a plot for fifteen dollars. Dr. Crawford's body was disinterred and buried alongside Naomi in the new family plot.[14]

> Mr. Nicholls' daughter, Miss Mary A. Nicholls of McDonnel Street, remembers those gentle retiring people who loved beauty so much and money so little. She has tales to tell of the poet, Isabella, who stood so straight when she walked, in the manner of an older time, who had such pretty light brown hair and lovely blue eyes "the eyes that came from

Ireland" and who was such a brilliant conversationalist in company.

"It seems like a cloudy day, ladies," said Isabella on one occasion with a whimsical smile, when Miss Nicholls and her sister went to visit the Crawford home, wearing long 'clouds' wrapped about them. But it was a heartbroken note that echoed in the bright voice when she stood beside the coffin of her younger sister, who passed away at the age of twenty years. As Isabella stood by the casket she said: "I will be the last to look on her face."[15]

How many graves had Isabella wept over? The little ones all those long years ago in Ireland. She was five years old. The little ones who died in Canada when they first came out. Then her father, and six months later, the sweet Naomi.

> Where's speech in anguish? O she never throve
> On the high swell of Sorrow's bursting heart.
> Two groans are hers that give themselves to speech
> "God, God!" with this she wails Him up before
> Her Bar of Desolation—then, "Why? Why?"
> Spurts through her hollowed graves and empty shrines
> For who will fling the iron doors apart
> Where naked Sorrow sits, and free her shriek
> To beat in strength against the granite world?
>
> Hugh and Iron
> lines 143-151

It would be comforting to think that in Isabella's life there had been a romantic interest—some special person to whom she could turn for consolation and loving advice in those dark days. With her early biographers there is no allusion to romance, illicit or otherwise. But neither is there any hint of scandal involving Dr. Crawford's stint as Treasurer for the Township of Elderslie.

It is Dorothy Livesay who first causes speculation about a possible involvement with the Reverend Vincent Clementi. This talented musician and the first president of the Mechanics' Institute in Lakefield is referred to by Livesay as a "new vicar, youthful, vigorous."[16] Existing photographs would contradict that description. Clementi was born in 1812. He would be fifty-one years old when he arrived in Lakefield while Isabella was just thirteen. A romantic relationship between these two would be most unlikely.

Dorothy Farmiloe says Livesay may have confused Vincent with his son, Theodore, who was a land surveyor, and married to his stepsister with whom he was raised.[17] Penny Petrone states: "There is no documentary evidence of any friendship between Crawford and Clementi, who had come to Canada from England (1855) where his father, Muzio Clementi, 'Father of the Pianoforte,' was a celebrated composer, but we see in Crawford's later works a marked interest in music and a love of Italy."[18]

And what of Isabella? If not Clementi (the elder or younger), the sexually explicit imagery of her poetry, in particular *The Lily Bed*, would lead us to believe she had been involved with someone in a passionate love affair; it is too explicit to ignore.

> I know the dainty spot
> (Ah, who doth know it not?)
> Where pure young Love his lily-cradle made,
> And nestled some sweet springs
> With lily-spangled wings—
> Forget-me-nots upon his bier I laid.
>
> The Hidden Room
> lines 25-30

His cedar paddle, scented, red,
He thrust down through the lily bed;

Cloaked in a golden pause he lay
Locked in the arms of the placid bay.

Trembled alone his bark canoe
As shocks of bursting lilies flew

...And he had spoke his soul of love
With voice of eagle and of dove.

Of loud, strong pines his tongue was made;
His lips, soft blossoms in the shade,

That kissed her silver lips—her's cool
As lilies on his inmost pool—

Till now he stood, in triumph's rest,
His image painted in her breast.

One isle 'tween blue and blue did melt,—
A bead of wampum from the belt

Of Manitou—a purple rise
On the far shore heaved to the skies.

His cedar paddle, scented, red,
He drew up from the lily bed.

The Lily Bed
lines 1-6
and 29-42

These were rather steamy lines to publish in Victorian times.

Other writers kept journals. Other writers kept little packets of letters, neatly tied with ribbon, letters from their friends and loved ones which they would read, and reread, then tuck away. Certainly Isabella would have corresponded with her brother in Algoma, with her Uncle John Irwin who sent them money, and with the Miss Valentine who came to visit in Lakefield and accompanies her when she called on Catherine Parr Traill. Were the contents of her letters and her journals so incriminating that they were destroyed by her mother, or some other well-meaning person who did not wish the poet's reputation tarnished? It is unlikely we shall ever know.

The time following the family deaths were dark days for Isabella and her mother. Once again, and for whatever reason, they changed their residence and moved into rooms above a grocery store at the corner of Aylmer and Hunter Streets.[19] Were they seeking cheaper accommodation (certainly there would have been a need to economize), or were they attempting to escape the house that held such sorrowful reminders? With Dr. Crawford and Naomi dead, and Stephen Walter once again in Algoma, nothing remained to hold them in Peterborough.

It is this writer's opinion that at this time they sold whatever furniture they had accumulated during their years in Canada and took furnished lodgings.

Only their very treasured possessions would accompany them on their next move, this time to Toronto.

Five

TORONTO

Toronto was a logical choice for Isabella Valancy Crawford. It was a sophisticated metropolis, the intellectual and cultural center of eastern English-speaking Canada. Of more importance, the newspapers publishing her work were in that city. Women who were writing, as well as men, found Toronto the core of the literary scene. Mrs. J.W.F. Harrison (Seranus) was the first musical, and then literary editor of *The Week*. Agnes Maude Machar (Fidelis) was writing novels, historical tales and poetry. Sara Jeanette Duncan wrote for *The Globe* and *The Week*, and, in 1888, became parliamentary correspondent of the *Montreal Star*. Pamela Vining Yule published *Poems of heart and home* in Toronto in 1881. Pauline Johnson was publishing and also Ethelwyn Wetherald who, in 1905, would write the introduction to *The Collected Poems of Isabella Valancy Crawford*.[1]

Isabella applied for membership in the Toronto Mechanics' Institute, and her signature appeared in the register June 20, 1876.[2] The Mechanics' Institute was housed in an impressive neoclassical building on Church Street at the corner of Adelaide. It boasted a semi-circular lecture theatre which rose in tiers from the basement to the first floor, a library with reading rooms and two grand

staircases leading to the second-floor music hall. With the
passage of the Free Library Bylaw in 1883, the Mechanics'
Institute was taken over by the city to form the basis of the
Toronto Public Library system. Part of the building was
altered, the music hall became the reading room with
large, newspaper holding-racks down the center. The pub-
lic library opened March 6, 1884. However, from the
beginning, the Mechanics' Institute held lectures on a
wide range of subjects which included literature, music,
natural and experimental science and astronomy. The
name was misleading as many of the members were pro-
fessional and business people.

How eagerly Isabella must have paid her two dollar
yearly fee and hastened to peruse the publications now
so readily available to her. Her address at this time was
142 Shuter Street. She and her mother had taken rooms
with a Miss J. Rutherford. This Miss Rutherford and her
sister entertained the Crawford ladies with stories, stories
that Isabella found sufficiently interesting to record.
Dreams and Manifestations and *Mrs. Hay's Ghost* were
found among her manuscripts and dated July 18, 1876.[3]

The city of Toronto was much more to their liking.
Mrs. Crawford was accustomed to city ways, and, as for
Isabella, well here on these busy downtown streets, she
could go about her business unheeded. Her shabby
appearance did not matter. She would not seem odd
among Toronto's motley crew. No children would follow
her and call out her name. There were no apartments as
we know them today. Boarding and rooming houses were
a natural haven for a widowed lady and her daughter, that
is, unless they had enough money to allow them to stay in
a residential hotel. Obviously the Crawfords did not. And
again, as in Peterborough, they frequently changed lodg-
ings.

From Dorothy Farmiloe's *Isabella Valancy Crawford*

—*The Life and the Legends,* [4] the Toronto addresses have been ascertained:

1876	142 Shuter Street	landlady, Miss J. Rutherford
1881	St. Andrews Ward	no other information
1882-1883	214 Adelaide West	landlady, Mrs. Harriet Farquharson
1884	180 Adelaide West	landlord, Thomas Carridice
1885	216 Adelaide West	landlady, Miss J. Harrison
1886	57 John cor. King	landlady, Mrs. Chas. J. Stuart

In this city, whose population was 86,415 in 1881, the Crawford ladies faced their future.

> She moves to meet the centuries, her feet
> All shod with emerald, and her light robe
> Fringed with leaves singing in the jazel air.
> Her tire is rich, not with stout battlements,
> Prophets of strife, but wealthy with tall spires
> All shining Godward, rare with learning's domes,
> And burning with young stars that promise suns
> To clasp her older brows. On her young breast
> Lie linked the fair, clear pearls of many homes,—
> Mightly and lovely chain, from its white strength
> Hangs on her heart the awful jewel, Hope.
>
> Toronto
> lines 1-11

From any one of their boarding houses they were able to see buildings of extraordinary beauty, magnificent buildings such as the Customs House, the second Union Station, Osgoode Hall, the McMaster Warehouse, Government House and on and on. All along Front Street, Adelaide, Yonge, King and Queen Streets were structures worthy of any European capital.

> On the south side, the "dollar" or fashionable side of King Street, continuously from York Street to the Market, are the spacious plate glass windows, glittering with jewelry, with gold and silver plate, with elaborate china and bric-a-brac, with sheen of satin-shining tissues for Toronto brides…. Here are restaurants, where men and ladies can dine in comfort, and as luxuriously as in any in New York or London, photographers, art warerooms. Is there any luxurious taste you desire to gratify, any decorative art you would pursue? In that case, o reader, "put money in thy purse," (for that is an indispensable condition), and take a walk along the south side of King Street.[5]

Isabella did not have money to put in her purse to avail herself of such luxuries, but the newly-grand King Street was there for her to see and important to her writing. All her efforts were in that direction. Her stories must be sold, her poems must find a market.

"Where Love, Art Hid" was published July 7, 1876 in *The National*.[6] *The Toronto Evening Telegram* was receptive and paid one to three dollars for each published piece. Her poems appeared in that newspaper almost every other week.[7]

As other writers of her time were doing, Isabella sometimes used a pseudonym. At the end of the draft manuscript *The Halton Boys*, we find written: "Denis Scott, General Post Office, Toronto, Ontario."[8] The fact that she used this pseudonym, and the possibility that she

may have used others, prevents researchers from deter-
mining the extent of her publications. Her short stories
and novellas were romantic and often melodramatic, but
they were what her readers wanted, and they sold.
Her prose works were published in Frank Leslie's
Popular Monthly, in *The Globe*, in *The Evening Globe*, and
in Frank Leslie's *Illustrated News*. Her poetry appeared in
The Favorite, *The Mail*, *The National*, *The Toronto Globe*,
and *The Evening Telegram*. She was a prolific writer, and
she counted every word. Throughout her unpublished
manuscripts can be found word counts and columns of
figures. She also listed markets, magazines and newspa-
pers, together with addresses—all scrawled on the pages
of an old copy book that once belonged to a young
Stephen Walter.[9]

> At that time, on narrow Jordan Street, a brilliant
> journal The Week had its beginning, founded by
> Goldwin Smith, with Charles G.D. Roberts as its first
> editor. The musical and literary editor was Mrs.
> J.W.F. Harrison (Seranus) who speaks of a new writer
> (Isabella) who climbed those dingy stairs: "A tall,
> dark young woman, one whom most people would
> feel was difficult almost repellent in her manner. But
> her work charmed me, though I had to tell her that
> we didn't pay for poetry."[10]

Difficult, repellent in manner—this is not the Isabella
we knew in Lakefield and Peterborough. It is interesting
to note that Isabella is now being described as tall and
dark. Elsewhere she is remembered as tall and fair, with
beautiful hair; and by one other account as short, dumpy
and unattractive:
Miss Crawford appeared to be about 30 years of age,
somewhat stout and a little below in average height. Her

dress was poor, at times almost shabby, and it was not until she spoke that one was at all impressed with her personality. Her features were not beautiful, but in conversation she lighted up and her eyes sparkled with vivacity to an unusual degree. She was a clever conversationalist, and her animation and her versatility made her a delightful companion.[11]

Life had hardened Isabella. From her photograph we can see that the mature Isabella lost the sweetness of face portrayed in her early likeness. In her thirties, her eyes held bitter acceptance, not dreams. Very aware of social ills, she saw poverty:

> With the inimitable wilderness around
> From the close city hives rang up the groan
> "So little space!—we starve—we faint, we die!"
> Lord! Lord! to see the gaping city sewer
> Beaded with haggard heads—and hungry eyes
> Peering above the heaving of the drains
> And hear the harsh, unreasonable cry
> "We starve, we starve!" While half a world lay fresh
> And teeming, out beyond the city gates!
>
> Hugh and Ion
> lines 199-207

She condemned British imperialism:

> Beat down the corn, tear up the vine,
> The waters turn to blood;
> And if the wretch for bread doth wine,
> Give him his kin for food.
> Ay, strew the dead to saddle-girth,
> They make so rich a mold,
> Thou wilt enrich the wasted earth—

They'll turn to yellow gold.
On with thy thunders! Shot and shell
Send screaming, featly hurled—
Science has made them in her cell
To civilize the world.

War
lines 9-20

Her passionate nature beat itself out in words, both passionate and sensuous. Consider these lines:

And through warm blackness fell the bless'd spring
balm
Of rain upon the world. All through the night
Life loos'd the awful fountain of his heart
And earth grew tremulous with pulsing seeds
And leaping stems, and juices rushing up
From her wide veins along the barren woods
And all the budding boughs in that short night,
Did dimple with small leaves a dew drop large.

Hugh and Ion
lines 269-276

In 1884 Isabella decided to publish a volume of her poetry. She collected forty-three poems and when she could not find anyone willing to assume the financial risk of such a publication, she approached James Bain and Son of Toronto, and commissioned them to print one thousand copies at her expense.

It was done! Her book was in print! *Old Spookses' Pass, Malcolm's Katie, and Other Poems* was 224 pages long and dedicated to her uncle, John Irwin Crawford. Fifty copies were bound in salmon-coloured wrappers and sent out to reviewers. Her hopes were high.

Reviews of the book appeared. Toronto newspaper

critics received it well and comments were favourable, but the response was not effusive. In England, however, her work was lauded: "Here is a volume that comes from a Country as yet unfertile of literature. If the harvest is as good as the first fruits, it will be well, for Miss Crawford writes with a power of expression quite unusual among aspirants of poetic fame."[12]

A copy of the book sent to Lord Dufferin, Governor General of Canada 1872-78, brought this response:[13]

> British Embassy
> Constantinople
> June 21, '84
>
> My dear Miss Crawford:
> It is really too good of you to have thought of sending me your book. It has just arrived and I have already read several of the beautiful poems it contains with very great pleasure. You are quite right in supposing that I still take the deepest interest in everything that concerns the welfare of Canada. It is time now that Canada should have a literature of its own, and I am glad to think that you should have so nobly shown the way.
> Believe me, my dear Miss Crawford, with received thanks, and with my best wishes for your future fame.
> Ever yours sincerely,
> (sdg) Dufferin

Isabella distributed her book, and placed an advertisement in *The Globe* which stated that it was available at all book dealers for fifty cents a copy.[14] Then she waited.

The publication was a failure. Only fifty copies of *Old Spookses' Pass, Malcolm's Katie and Other Poems* were ever sold. Why? The following are some of the reasons that

have been put forth. The book was too cheaply printed
and bound. It had not been properly proof-read and it
was full of errors. The title was exceedingly awkward.
Isabella was not sufficiently well-known, there had been
too little publicity, it was not properly edited and not
properly marketed. Whatever the reason, or reasons,
Isabella Valancy Crawford would not experience literary
fame in her lifetime.

In December 1885 Isabella and her mother moved
again, this time into rooms on the third floor of a build-
ing on the south-east corner of King and John Streets. A
few years ago, I went to Toronto specifically to visit this
building. The main floor was occupied by a restaurant,
The King's Plate, but the second floor and the third floor
were vacant, having just been newly-carpeted and painted.
The proprietor of the restaurant very kindly gave me the
key to the side entrance, which was the 57 John Street
address of the Crawfords (renumbered in 1890). I was
permitted to climb the stairs and stand in the rooms
where Isabella once lived. Though there was little to cap-
ture on film, I photographed the interior: the deep-silled
dormer windows that faced in four directions; and the
stairway, not as narrow as I had thought it would be, ris-
ing to a landing that had wainscoting on the wall and
attractive carving on the face boards. I felt a deep sense of
awe and was glad the rooms were unfurnished.

I stood in the window overlooking King Street. I
could see Ed's Warehouse and the Royal Alexandra
Theatre. The Crawfords would have seen Upper Canada
College in its first setting. My view to the east was of Roy
Thomson Hall with St. Andrew's Presbyterian Church in
the background. The church was there in 1885, but
Government House, with its elegant porte-cochere, gar-
den verandah and conservatory, occupied the site of the
concert hall, and the lieutenant governor was in residence.

From the window facing south I saw the C.N. Tower and the Convention Centre on Front Street. Isabella would have looked down on the Third Houses of Parliament, and beyond, the railway tracks and still farther to the waters of Lake Ontario.

In 1886 the *Toronto Evening Globe* accepted "A Little Bacchante; or Some Black Sheep" for publication in serial form. An article in *The Varsity* of Toronto on January 23, 1886 stated: "The novel by Isabella Valancy Crawford in *The Globe* is vastly superior to the ordinary run of newspaper fiction.[15]

Two years had passed since Isabella's volume *Old Spookses' Pass, Malcolm's Katie and Other Poems* appeared on the market. Because of the favourable publicity coming from "The Little Bacchante" the time was right to re-issue her poetry, or so she felt. Isabella supplied a new title page which omitted the publishers' imprint, James Bain & Son (including the date), and placed her own name, the words, *"Author of A Little Bacchante; or Some Black Sheep."* This new volume was issued in gray or blue paper boards.[16]

She did not lose hope, but sometimes the days seemed very dark, and the future very bleak.

> Without the West drew flaming gates across
> The grey, gaunt distance of the wintry street
> Low down were welded fast against the sky
> Dull, purple bars that held the first, fine snow.
> Lower, the old unutterable pray'r
> That glows in golden script behind the day
> Stretched its still strength about the dark'ning world
> And as a cobweb delicately spun
> Bare black thin boughs hung orb'd against the sky
> And in their subtle lacings seem'd to cling
> Arachne-like, the round, full Evening Star.

Dark on near hills the primal forest heav'd
Its haughty heart against the City's claws
That lengthen'd towards its ramparts day by day;
Dark on near sands the tideless waters stood
Meek with dun mist—moaning against wan wharves
Dying to dumbness as the fierce young frost
Gaz'd on the shuddering world, ere serpent-wise
He coil'd chill crystal folds about its breast.
On such an eve despair seems no strange growth
But a chief vein that feeds the chilling heart,
With pausing billows stiff'ning as they burst
And Hope an alien flame fall'n from the wick
Of a cold lamp that chills the failing hand.
Dust, sharp as spear points in the rising frost
Whirl'd in keen simoons, and, sullen orbs
The base stars of the city lamps, leap'd up.

Hugh and Ion
lines 116-142

Isabella and her mother had always been close. An early biographer told us: "Never had author more responsive listener than Mrs. Crawford proved to be to her daughter, laughing over her wit, entering into her moods and fancies, and like the mother of old, hoarding up in her heart all the sayings of her child.[17] They had been through a lot together, now in these Toronto years Isabella looked to her mother for companionship, and help as well, in copying her manuscripts for submission.[18]

In the summer of 1886 something happened to brighten their lives. On July 25 Stephen Walter married Eliza Jane Arnhill of Paisley, Ontario in a ceremony which took place in Iron Bridge, Ontario. Stephen Walter brought his bride to Toronto to meet his mother and his sister.

They would have arrived in the city by train at the

second Union Station on Front Street and, perhaps, because it was their wedding trip, they stayed at either the American or the Queen's Hotel. In any case they would have gone to see the fashionable Queen's that served such guests as Lord Dufferin; Grand Duke Alexis of Russia; Jefferson Davis, the President of the Confederacy and General Sherman (who burnt Atlanta in 1865). The Royal York Hotel now stands on the site of the Queen's Hotel.

Isabella and her mother must have enjoyed showing off their city. Possibly they visited the Grand Opera House on Adelaide Street which had been rebuilt following damage by fire, attended a church service in one of Toronto's magnificent places of worship, saw the Crystal Palace at the Exhibition Grounds and rode on horse-drawn streetcars on streets which, since 1884, were lit with stream-generated electricity. Maybe they saw a cricket match, or took the ferry to Toronto Island to have lunch at the Hotel Hanlan and watch the boaters from the Toronto Yacht Club.

Toronto in 1886 was an exciting and wonderful city. The Timothy Eaton and Robert Simpson stores were competing for trade at the corner of Queen and Yonge and there were telephones in both stores. Simpson's served tea to the ladies, but Eaton's provided a children's nurse. The A.R. McMaster Warehouse, built in 1871 at 12 Front Street, was serviced by an Otis steam-driven elevator. So much to see! And just one block away from the Crawfords were the four corners of King and Simcoe Streets, which then contained Government House, Upper Canada College, St. Andrew's Church, and a saloon. What did Toronto residents call these corners? They had been 'respectively dubbed' Legislation, Education, Salvation and Damnation.[19]

Stephen Walter and Eliza Jane returned to the north. Mrs. Crawford and Isabella settled back into their routine.

What had Isabella's reaction been to the presence of young wedded bliss? She would soon be thirty-six years old. For her there would not be an ardent lover, husband. Were there tears in the night?

For oh, the passionate Isabella:

Dawn swam the east; against her breast the night
Broke purple, and her curving arms beat back
The starry surf—she reach'd the shining shoals
And slipp'd the crimson of her lusty foot
On the firm ground and from her breast and knee
Her opal shoulder, and the ruddy palms
That smote the misty tresses from her eyes
Light fell, in half heard music, on the earth.
Naked, a second, on the shore she stood
With all the innocent, small feather'd things
Flying to touch the scarlet, lucid bars
Of her stretch'd fingers, and against her knees
Rubb'd the soft sides of shadowy deer, and high
The squirrels chatter'd at her from rich boughs
Then warmer wound the blood wide in her veins.
She mov'd an ardent palm, and drew the mists
From lakes, and swamps and valleys; and their folds
Spic'd with the cedar and the balsam—bright
On their curl'd edges with a saffron dye
She upward drew along her rosy knees
Her ivory thighs, the silver of her breast,
So veil'd and drap'd she waited for the sun.

Hugh and Ion
lines 350-372

Evidence of a growing bitterness and disillusionment surfaces in a letter written by Isabella to the editor of *Arcturus* in 1887

I feel that I should wish to introduce myself to your notice as a possible contributor to the pages of Arcturus. Of course the possibility is remote as by some chance no contribution of mine has ever been accepted by any first-class Canadian literary journal. I have contributed to the Mail and Globe, and won some very kind words from eminent critics, but have been quietly "sat upon" by the High Priests of Canadian periodical literature. I am not very seriously injured by the process, and indeed there have lately been signs of relenting on the part of the powers that be, as I was offered an extended notice of my book in the column of the...and the.... This proposal I declined (I suppose judiciously), as I think it might have been given at first, instead of coming in late in the day, and at the heels of warm words from higher literary authorities.[20]

The opinions expressed in this letter reveal the extent of her injured feelings: her work was not appreciated as she felt it ought to be, and she was angry.

Toward the end of January 1887, Isabella developed a bad cold. Instead of looking after herself by resting and staying indoors, she continued to trudge through the slushy streets in a Toronto known for its penetrating chill in winter. She had to deliver her poems to her newspaper publishers and she must make her endless trips to the General Post Office some blocks away on Adelaide Street East. There just possibly, an envelope would await her containing a cheque in payment of some piece she had written, or a notice of acceptance, not rejection. Disregarding her mother's remonstrances, she spent longer hours each evening at her writing table.

On the night of February 12, 1887 Isabella was

preparing for bed. About eleven-thirty she experienced a sharp and suffocating pain in her chest and called to her mother in alarm. Mrs. Crawford cried out for Mrs. Stuart to come upstairs, and it was the landlady who held Isabella and heard her last words, "What a trouble I am, Mrs. Stuart." At the age of thirty-six, Isabella Valancy Crawford was dead.[21]

Her untimely death touched those few who had at times been close to her. Mrs. A. J. Heffernan, formerly Miss Stuart, said:

> I was a young girl at the time of her death but how could I forget one like Miss Crawford? She seemed like a being from another planet. There was something about her that the world in general could not be expected to understand. She and her mother lived almost completely by themselves during the years that they lodged with us, except for one or two friends. But they had their own pursuits. They were deeply interested in English and European literature, and would speak French together constantly. Miss Crawford always liked me to practice my school-girl French with her. I used to watch her make her wonderful Irish potato cakes in our kitchen while she described the whole process to me in the language I was trying so hard to learn. I think she was really gay at heart, but at times seemed sad and depressed. Her passion for music was almost as great as her love for books and poetry. She studied the piano and played very well indeed, collecting a good deal of music, a part of which she gave to me.... And there were things to charm a young girl in the two little rooms upstairs. I remember a flounce of precious old lace, and chintzes, and quaint ornaments, and an Indian prayer rug, Miss Crawford's special treasure sent to her by

her uncle, Dr. John Irwin Crawford, a Royal Navy officer who was much on the Indian seas... . Miss Crawford was not exactly beautiful, but I shall never forget the wonderful animation of her face at times, and its sadness in repose.[22]

Among the Crawford friends was a Mrs. Donald Urquhart in whose hospitable home there was always a warm welcome during the Toronto years.

"I remember as though it were yesterday, this girl whose life was always creative, and always drawn to far-away and exquisitely suggestive things. She would forget all her failures and discouragements when she was at the piano, or composing poetry or stories. Then—there was a strange thing!—she had a great delight in cutting out and making the most unique and beautiful little foreign figures, tiny dolls, always of oriental types, made out of vivid coloured silks or satins; Rajahs and Mandarins and Hindoo priests in their robes and turbans, with their attendants perfectly costumed. She would spend hours over these things, making every detail correct. They were arranged on a silk-covered cardboard stage half the size of my dining-room table. She could not afford to have her poems well bound," continued Mrs. Urquhart, "so she made a special cover for ours, knowing how much my husband and I appreciated her work."

And I held in my hand "Old Spookses' Pass" in faded peacock blue satin, covered with fine rose-point lace.[23]

This embroidered sculpture of her work was given to Hugh Garton, a young boy who was ill. His parents were friends of Stephen Walter, and to them Isabella presented a volume of her poetry, which is inscribed by her, and now in the archives of the Peterborough Public Library.[24] Hugh Garton in 1954, when he was 80 years of age, gave the tableau to the Peterborough Historical Society, and it is now in the possession of the Peterborough Centennial Museum. It is carefully stored, but the materials are rotting, and the coloured silks are fading. I was recently informed by Kenneth Doherty, Director, that further conservation is being considered.

Isabella's last poem to appear in print while she was alive was published in the Toronto *Telegram* on February 5, 1887. It was entitled "The Rose of a Nation's Thanks" and commemorated the return of soldier volunteers from the Northwest Rebellion. It had first appeared June 11, 1885 but was republished at the request of *Telegram* readers, only one week before her death.

> A Welcome? There is not a babe at the breast won't
>   spring at the roll of the drum
> That heralds them home—the keen, long cry in the air
>   of "They come! They come!"
> And what of it all if ye bade them wade knee-deep in a
>   wave of wine,
> And tossed tall torches, and arched the town in garlands
>   of maple and pine?
> All dust in the wind of a woman's cry as she snatches
>   from the ranks
> Her boy who bears on his bold young breast the Rose
>   of a Nation's Thanks!
>
>   The Rose of a Nation's Thanks
>   lines 25-36

A funeral service was held for Isabella in Toronto at

2 p.m. on Tuesday, February 15, 1887 and her body was temporarily placed in a vault at the Necropolis, to be removed on March 4, and taken to Peterborough's Little Lake Cemetery for interment in the family plot. Among the floral tributes at her funeral was a single great white bloom with an unsigned card bearing this message: "The Rose of a Nation's Thanks."[25]

On February 14, 1887 *The Evening Telegram* published an obituary which contained these remarks: "Miss Crawford was a young lady of marked ability and native wit, and had already made her mark in the world of literature, poetry, as well as prose.

The Globe ran two notices of her death—one on February 14, and another on February 15. From February 14: "...She was well-known to readers of *The Globe* as the writer of 'The Little Bacchante' together with several poems of extraordinary merit. For several years she had written for leading American and English newspapers, and published one volume of poems which received the highest commendation from literary journals."

And on February 15: "The death of Isabella Valancy Crawford, which took place at 11:30 on Saturday night, was the result of heart disease and quite unlooked for. Miss Crawford had been suffering from a cold for a fortnight past, but had not been confined to bed.... About ten years ago a medical man gave it as his opinion that the action of the deceased lady's heart was defective, and as the complaint was hereditary... Miss Crawford was always careful to avoid over-exertion."

For years her body lay in an unmarked grave. Then in 1899, through the efforts of the Peterborough Historical Society and Kit of *The Mail and Empire* (Kathleen Blake Coleman), a drive for funds was organized. Donations were credited in *The Mail and Empire* for amounts ranging from ten cents to one dollar.[26]

On November 2, 1900 her friends erected above her grave, a six-foot celtic cross of grey Canadian granite. It bears the inscription:

Isabella Valancy Crawford
Poet
By the Gift of God

...but toward the sun
The eagle lifts his eyes, and with his wings
Beats on a sunlight that is never marred
By cloud, or mist, shrieks his fierce joy to air
Ne'er stirred by stormy pulse.
The eagle mine, I said, "Oh I would ride
His wings like Ganymede, nor ever care
To drop upon the stormy earth again
But circle star-ward, narrowing my gyres
To some great planet of eternal peace."

Between the Wind and Rain
lines 28-37

ISABELLA VALANCY CRAWFORD
A Selected Anthology of Poetry

The poetry contained in the Selected Anthology has been chosen to reflect what, to the author, represents Crawford's progression from simple romantic lyricism to a realism and an awareness of Canadian landscape, pioneer existance and Indian legend. What surfaces here is her deep social conscience and concern, unforgettably articulated in vigorous and powerful blank verse that is unmistakably Canadian.

SAID THE DAISY

There ne'er was blown out of the yellow east
    So fresh, so fair, so sweet a morn as this.
The dear earth decked herself as for a feast;
    And, as for me, I trembled with my bliss.
The young grass round me was so rich with dew,
    And sang me such sweet, tender strains, as low
The breath of dawn among its tall spikes blew;
    But what it sang none but myself can know!

O never came so glad a morn before!
    So rosy dimpling burst the infant light,
So crystal pure the air the meadows o'er,
    The lark with such young rapture took his flight,
The round world seemed not older by an hour
    Than mine own daisy self! I laughed to see
How, when her first red roses paled and died,
    The blue sky smiled, and decked her azure lea
With daisy clouds, white, pink-fringed, just like me!

"This is the morn for song," sang out the lark,
    "O silver-tressed beloved!" My golden eye
Watched his brown wing blot out the last star-spark
    Amidst the daisy cloudlets of the sky.

"No morn so sweet as this, so pure, so fair—
    God's bud time" so the oldest white thorn said,
And she has lived so long; yet here and there
    Such fresh white buds begem her ancient head.

And from her thorny bosom all last night
    Deep in my dew-sealed sleep I heard a note—
So sweet a voice of anguish and delight
    I dreamed a red star had a bird-like throat
And that its rays were music which had crept
    'Mid the white-scented blossoms of the thorn,
And that to hear her sing the still night wept
    With mists and dew until the yellow morn.

I wonder, wonder what the song he sang,
    That seemed to drown in melody the vales!
I knew my lark's song as he skyward sprang,
    But only roses know the nightingale's.
The yellow cowslip bent her honeyed lips
    And whispered: "Daisy, wert thou but as high
As I am, thou couldst see the merry ships
    On yon blue wondrous field blown gaily by."

A gay, small wind, arch as a ruddy fox,
    Crept round my slender, green and dainty stem,
And piped: "Let me but shake thy silver locks
    And free thy bent head from its diadem
Of diamond dew, and thou shalt rise and gaze,
    Like the tall cowslips, o'er the rustling grass,
On proud, high cliffs, bright strands and sparkling bays,
    And watch the white ships as they gaily pass."

"Oh, while thou mayst keep thou thy crystal dew!"
    Said the aged thorn, where sang the heart of
    night,

The nightingale. "The sea is very blue,
      The sails of ships are wondrous swift and white.
Soon, soon enough thy dew will sparkling die,
      And thou, with burning brow and thirsty lips,
Wilt turn the golden circle of thine eye,
      Nor joy in them, on ocean and her ships!"

There never flew across the violet hills
      A morn so like a dove with jewelled eyes,
With soft wings fluttering like the sound of rills,
      And gentle breast of rose and azure dyes.
The purple trumpets of the clover sent
      Such rich, dew-loosened perfume, and the bee
Hung like a gold drop in the woodbine's tent.
      What care I for the gay ships and the sea!

THE ROSE

The Rose was given to man for this:
      He, sudden seeing it in later years,
Should swift remember Love's first lingering kiss
      And Grief's last lingering tears;

Or, being blind, should feel its yearning soul
      Knit all its piercing perfume round his own,
Till he should see on memory's ample scroll
      All roses he had known;

Or, being hard, perchance his finger-tips
      Careless might touch the satin of its cup,
And he should feel a dead babe's budding lips
      To his lips lifted up;

Or, being deaf and smitten with its star,
      Should, on a sudden, almost hear a lark
Rush singing up—the nightingale afar
      Sing thro' the dew-bright dark;

Or, sorrow-lost in paths that round and round
      Circle old graves, its keen and vital breath
Should call to him within the yew's bleak bound
      Of Life, and not of Death.

THE MOTHER'S SOUL

When the moon was horned the mother died,
      And the child pulled at her hand and knee,
And he rubbed her cheek and loudly cried:
      "O mother, arise, give bread to me!"
      But the pine tree bent its head,
      And the wind at the door-post said:
      "O child, thy mother is dead!"

The sun set his loom to weave the day;
      The frost bit sharp like a silent cur;
The child by her pillow paused in his play:
      "Mother, build up the sweet fire of fir!"
      But the fir tree shook its cones,
      And loud cried the pitiful stones:
      "Wolf Death has thy mother's bones!"

They bore the mother out on her bier;
      Their tears made warm her breast and shroud;
The smiling child at her head stood near;
      And the long, white tapers shook and bowed,

And said with their tongues of gold,
To the icy lumps of the brave mold:
"How heavy are ye and cold!"

They buried the mother; to the feast
They flocked with the beaks of unclean crows.
The wind came up from the red-eyed east
And bore in its arms the chill, soft snows.
They said to each other: "Sere
Are the hearts the mother held dear;
Forgotten, her babe plays here!"

The child with the tender snow flakes played,
And the wind on its fingers twined his hair;
And still by the tall, brown grave he stayed,
Alone in the churchyard lean and bare.
The sods on the high grave cried
To the mother's white breast inside:
"Lie still; in thy deep rest bide!"

Her breast lay still like a long-chilled stone,
Her soul was out on the bleak, grey day;
She saw her child by the grave alone,
With the sods and snow and wind at play.
Said the sharp lips of the rush,
"Red as thy roses, O bush,
With anger the dead can blush!"

A butterfly to the child's breast flew,"
Fluttered its wings on his sweet, round cheek,
Danced by his fingers, small, cold and blue.
The sun strode down past the mountain peak,
The butterfly whispered low
To the child: "Babe, follow me: know,
Cold is earth here below."

The butterfly flew; followed the child,
    Lured by the snowy torch of its wings;
The wind sighed after them soft and wild
    Till the stars wedded night with golden rings;
    Till the frost upreared its head,
    And the ground to it groaned and said:
    "The feet of the child are lead!"

The child's head drooped to the brown, sere mold,
    On the crackling cones his white breast lay;
The butterfly touched the locks of gold,
    The soul of the child sprang from its clay.
    The moon to the pine tree stole,
    And, silver-lipped, said to its bole:
    "How strong is the mother's soul!"

The wings of the butterfly grew out
    To the mother's arms, long, soft and white;
She folded them warm her babe about,
    She kissed his lips into berries bright,
    She warmed his soul on her breast;
    And the east called out to the west:
    "Now the mother's soul will rest!"

Under the roof where the burial feast
    Was heavy with meat and red with wine,
Each crossed himself as out of the east
    A strange wind swept over oak and pine.
    The trees to the home-roof said:
    " 'Tis but the airy rush and tread
    Of angels greeting thy dead."

*In Eastern Europe, the soul of the deceased is said to hover, in the shape of a bird or butterfly, close to the body until after the burial.

HIS CLAY

He died; he was buried, the last of his race,
And they laid him away in his burial-place.

And he said in his will, "When I have done
With this mask of clay that I have on,

"Bury it simply—I'm done with it,
At best is only a poor misfit.

"It cramped my brains and chained my soul,
And it clogged my feet as I sought my goal.

"When my soul and I were inclined to shout
O'er some noble thought we had chiseled out;

"When we'd polished the marble until it stood
So fair that we truly said: ' 'Tis good!'

"My soul would tremble, my spirit quail,
For it fell to the flesh to uplift the veil.

"It took our thought in its hands of clay,
And lo! how the beauty had passed away.

"When love came in to abide with me,
I said, 'Welcome, Son of Eternity!'

"I built him an altar strong and white,
Such as might stand in God's own sight;

"I chanted his glorious litany—
Pure Love is the Son of Eternity;

"But ever my altar shook alway
'Neath the brute hands of the tyrant clay.
"Its voice, with its accents harsh and drear,
Mocked at my soul and wailed in its ear:

" 'Why tend the altar and bend the knee?
Love lives and dies in the dust with me.'

"So the flesh that I wore chanced ever to be
Less of my friend than my enemy.

"Is there a moment this death-strong earth
Thrills, and remembers her time of birth?

"Is there a time when she knows her clay
As a star in the coil of the astral way?

"Who may tell? But the soul in its clod
Knows in swift moments its kinship to God—

"Quick lights in its chambers that flicker alway
Before the hot breath of the tyrant clay.

"So the flesh that I wore chanced ever to be
Less of my friend than my enemy.

"So bury it deeply—strong foe, weak friend—
And bury it cheaply, —and there its end!"

THE CAMP OF SOULS

My white canoe, like the silvery air
     O'er the River of Death that darkly rolls

When the moons of the world are round and fair,
    I paddle back from the "Camp of Souls."
When the wishton-wish in the low swamp grieves
Come the dark plumes of red "Singing Leaves."

Two hundred times have the moons of spring
    Rolled over the bright bay's azure breath
Since they decked me with plumes of an eagle's wing,
    And painted my face with the "paint of death,"
And from their pipes o'er my corpse there broke
The solemn rings of the blue "last smoke."

Two hundred times have the wintry moons
    Wrapped the dead earth in a blanket white;
Two hundred times have the wild sky loons
    Shrieked in the flush of the golden light
Of the first sweet dawn, when the summer weaves
Her dusky wigwam of perfect leaves.

Two hundred moons of the falling leaf
    Since they laid my bow in my dead right hand
And chanted above me the "song of grief"
    As I took my way to the spirit land;
Yet when the swallow the blue air cleaves
Comes the dark plumes of red "Singing Leaves."

White are the wigwams in that far camp,
    And the star-eyed deer on the plains are found;
No bitter marshes or tangled swamp
    In the Manitou's happy hunting-ground!
And the moon of summer forever rolls
Above the red men in their "Camp of Souls."

Blue are its lakes as the wild dove's breast,
    And their murmurs soft as her gentle note;

As the calm, large stars in the deep sky rest,
    The yellow lilies upon them float;
And canoes, like flakes of the silvery snow,
Thro' the tall, rustling rice-beds come and go.

Green are its forests; no warrior wind
    Rushes on war trail the dusk grove through,
With leaf-scalps of tall trees mourning behind;
    But South Wind, heart friend of Great Manitou,
When ferns and leaves with cool dew are wet,
Blows flowery breaths from his red calumet.

Never upon them the white frosts lie,
    Nor glow their green boughs with the "paint of
        death";
Manitou smiles in the crystal sky,
    Close breathing above them His life-strong
        breath;
And He speaks no more in fierce thunder sound,
So near is His happy hunting-ground.

Yet often I love in my white canoe,
    To come to the forests and camps of earth;
'Twas there death's black arrow pierced me through;
    'Twas there my red-browed mother gave me
        birth;
There I, in the light of a young man's dawn,
Won the lily heart of dusk "Springing Fawn."

And love is a cord woven out of life,
    And dyed in the red of the living heart;
And time is the hunter's rusty knife,
    That cannot cut the red strands apart:
And I sail from the spirit shore to scan
Where the weaving of that strong cord began.

But I may not come with a giftless hand,
  So richly I pile, in my white canoe,
Flowers that bloom in the spirit land.
  Immortal smiles of Great Manitou.
When I paddle back to the shores of earth
I scatter them over the white man's hearth.

For love is the breath of the soul set free;
  So I cross the river that darkly rolls,
That my spirit may whisper soft to thee
  Of *thine* who wait in the "Camp of Souls."
When the bright day laughs, or the wan night grieves,
Comes the dusky plumes of red "Singing Leaves."

THE SONG OF THE ARROW

What know I
As I bite the blue veins of the throbbing sky,
To the quarry's breast,
Hot from the sides of the sleek, smooth nest?

What know I
Of the will of the tense bow from which I fly?
What the need or jest
That feathers my flight to its bloody rest?

What know I
Of the will of the bow that speeds me on high?
What doth the shrill bow
Of the hand on its singing soul-string know?

Flame-swift speed I,
And the dove and the eagle shriek out and die.
Whence comes my sharp zest
For the heart of the quarry? The gods know best.

from: Gisli, The Chieftain
Part III

What time fierce Winter, like a wolf all lean,
       With sharp, white fangs bit at weak woodland
       things,
       Pierced furry breasts, and broke small painted
       wings,
And from dim homes all interlocked and green
Drove little spirits—those who love glossed leaves
       And glimmer in tall grasses—those who ride
       Glossed bubbles on the woodland's sheltered
       tide,
And make blue hyacinths their household eaves.

from: The Legend of the Mistletoe
lines 33 - 40

BETWEEN THE WIND AND RAIN

"The storm is in the air," she said, and held
Her soft palm to the breeze; and, looking up,
Swift sunbeams brushed the crystal of her eyes,
As swallows leave the skies to skim the brown,
Bright, woodland lakes. "The rain is in the air.

O Prophet Wind, what hast thou told the rose
That suddenly she loosens her red heart
And sends long perfumed sighs about the place?
O Prophet Wind, what hast thou told the swift
That from the airy eave she, shadow-grey,
Smites the blue pond and speeds her glancing wing
Close to the daffodils? What has thou told small bells
And tender buds that—all unlike the rose—
They draw green leaves close, close about their breasts
And shrink to sudden slumber? The sycamores
In every leaf are eloquent with thee,
The poplars busy all their silver tongues
With answering thee, and the round chestnut stirs
Vastly but softly at they prophecies.
The vines grow dusky with a deeper green
And with their tendrils snatch thy passing harp
And keep it by brief seconds in their leaves.

"O Prophet Wind, thou tellest of the rain,
While jacinth-blue, the broad sky folds calm palms,
Unwitting of all storm, high o'er the land!
The little grasses and the ruddy heath
Know of the coming rain; but toward the sun
The eagle lifts his eyes, and with his wings
Beats on a sunlight that is never marred
By cloud or mist, shrieks his fierce joy to air
Ne'er stirred by stormy pulse."
"The eagle mine," I said, "Oh, I would ride
His wings like Ganymede, nor ever care
To drop upon the stormy earth again,
But circle star-ward, narrowing my gyres
To some great planet of eternal peace."

"Nay," said my wise, young love, "the eagle falls
Back to his cliff, swift as a thunder-bolt;

For there his mate and naked eaglets dwell,
And there he rends the dove, and joys in all
The fierce delights of his tempestuous home;
And tho' the stormy earth throbs thro' her poles,
And rocks with tempests on her circling path,
And bleak, black clouds snatch at her purple hills,
While mate and eaglets shriek upon the rock,
The eagle leaves the hylas to its calm,
Beats the wild storm apart that rings the earth,
And seeks his eyrie on the wind-dashed cliff.
O Prophet Wind, close, close the storm and rain!"

Long swayed the grasses like a rolling wave
Above an undertow; the mastiff cried;
Low swept the poplars, groaning in their hearts;
And iron-footed stood the gnarled oaks,
And braced their woody thews against the storm.
Lashed from the pond, the ivory cygnets sought
The carven steps that plunged into the pool;
The peacocks screamed and dragged forgotten plumes;
On the sheer turf all shadows subtly died
In one large shadow sweeping o'er the land;
Bright windows in the ivy blushed no more;
The ripe, red walls grew pale, the tall vane dim.

Like a swift offering to an angry god,
O'erweighted wines shook plum and apricot
From trembling trellis, and the rose trees poured
A red libation of sweet, ripened leaves
On the trim walks; to the high dove-cote set
A stream of silver wings and violet breasts,
The hawk-like storm down swooping on their track.
"Go," said my love, "the storm would whirl me off
As thistle-down. I'll shelter there, but you—
You love no storms!"

"Where'er thou art," I said,
"Is all the calm I know. Wert thou enthroned
In maelstrom or on pivot of the winds,
Thou holdest in thy hand my palm of peace;
And, like the eagle, I would break the belts
Of shouting tempests to return to thee,
Were I above the storm on mighty wings
Yet no she-eagle thou! a small, white girl
I clasp and lift and carry from the rain
Across the windy lawn."
      With this I wove
Her floating lace about her floating hair
And crushed her snowy raiment to my breast,
And while she thought of frowns, but smiled instead,
And wrote her heart in crimson on her cheeks,
I bounded with her up the breezy slopes,
The storm about us with such airy din,
As of a thousand bugles, that my heart
Took courage in the clamour, and I laid
My lips upon the flower of her pink ear,
And said, "I love thee; give me love again!"
And here she paled,—love has its dread,—and then
She clasped its joy and reddened in its light,
Till all the daffodils I trod were pale
Beside the small flower red upon my breast.

And ere the dial on the slope was passed,
Between the last loud bugle of the Wind
And the first silver coinage of the rain
Upon my flying hair, there came her kiss
Gentle and pure upon my face—and thus
Were we betrothed between the wind and rain.

SAID THE CANOE

My masters twain made me a bed
Of pine-boughs resinous, and cedar;
Of moss, a soft and gentle breeder
Of dreams of rest; and me they spread
With furry skins and, laughing, said:
"Now she shall lay her polished sides
As queens do rest, or dainty brides,
Our slender lady of the tides!"

My masters twain their camp-soul lit;
Streamed incense from the hissing cones;
Large crimson flashes grew and whirled;
Thin golden nerves of sly light curled
Round the dun camp; and rose faint zones,
Half way about each grim bole knit,
Like a shy child that would bedeck
With its soft clasp a Brave's red neck,
Yet sees the rough shield on his breast,
The awful plumes shake on his crest,
And, fearful, drops his timid face,
Nor dares complete the sweet embrace.

Into the hollow hearts of brakes—
Yet warm from sides of does and stags
Passed to the crisp, dark river-flags—
Sinuous, red as copper-snakes,
Sharp-headed serpents, made of light,
Glided and hid themselves in night.

My masters twain the slaughtered deer
Hung on forked boughs with thongs of leather;
Bound were his stiff, slim feet together,
his eyes like dead stars cold and drear.

The wandering firelight drew near
And laid its wide palm, red and anxious,
On the sharp splendour of his branches,
On the white foam grown hard and sere
          On flank and shoulder.
Death—hard as breast of granite boulder—
          Under his lashes
Peered thro' his eyes at his life's grey ashes.

My masters twain sang songs that wove—
As they burnished hunting-blade and rifle—
A golden thread with a cobweb trifle,
Loud of the chase and low of love:
"O Love! art thou a silver fish,
Shy of the line and shy of gaffing,
Which we do follow, fierce, yet laughing,
Casting at thee the light-winged wish?
And at the last shall we bring thee up
From the crystal darkness, under the cup
          Of lily folden
          On broad leaves golden?

"O Love! art thou a silver deer
With feet as swift as wing of swallow,
While we with rushing arrows follow?
And at the last shall we draw near
And o'er thy velvet neck cast thongs
Woven of roses, stars and songs—
          New chains all moulden
          Of rare gems olden?"

They hung the slaughtered fish like swords
          On saplings slender; like scimitars,
          Bright, and ruddied from new-dead wars,
Blazed in the light the scaly hordes.

They piled up boughs beneath the trees,
      Of cedar web and green fir tassel.
      Low did the pointed pine tops rustle,
The camp-fire blushed to the tender breeze.

The hounds laid dewlaps on the ground
      With needles of pine, sweet, soft and rusty,
      Dreamed of the dead stag stout and lusty;
A bat by the red flames wove its round.

The darkness built its wigwam walls
      Close round the camp, and at its curtain
      Pressed shapes, thin, woven and uncertain
As white locks of tall waterfalls.

THE LILY BED

His cedar paddle, scented, red,
He thrust down through the lily bed;

Cloaked in a golden pause he lay,
Locked in the arms of the placid bay.

Trembled alone his bark canoe
As shocks of bursting lilies flew

Thro' the still crystal of the tide,
And smote the frail boat's birchen side;

Or, when beside the sedges thin
Rose the sharp silver of a fin;

Or when, a wizard swift and cold,
A dragon-fly beat out in gold

And jewels all the widening rings
Of waters singing to his wings;

Or, like a winged and burning soul,
Dropped from the gloom an oriole

On the cool wave, as to the balm
Of the Great Spirit's open palm

The freed soul flies. And silence clung
To the still hours, as tendrils hung,

In darkness carven, from the trees,
Sedge-buried to their burly knees.

Stillness sat in his lodge of leaves;
Clung golden shadows to its eaves,

And on its cone-spiced floor, like maize,
Red-ripe, fell sheaves of knotted rays.

The wood, a proud and crested brave;
Bead-bright, a maiden, stood the wave.

And he had spoke his soul of love
With voice of eagle and of dove.

Of loud, strong pines his tongue was made;
His lips, soft blossoms in the shade,

That kissed her silver lips—her's cool
As lilies on his inmost pool—

Till now he stood, in triumph's rest,
His image painted in her breast.

One isle 'tween blue and blue did melt,—
A bead of wampum from the belt

Of Manitou—a purple rise
On the far shore heaved to the skies.

His cedar paddle, scented, red,
He drew up from the lily bed;

All lily-locked, all lily-locked,
His light bark in the blossoms rocked.

Their cool lips round the sharp prow sang,
Their soft clasp to the frail sides sprang,

With breast and lip they wove a bar.
Stole from her lodge the Evening Star;

With golden hand she grasped the mane
Of a red cloud on her azure plain.

It by the peaked, red sunset flew;
Cool winds from its bright nostrils blew.

They swayed the high, dark trees, and low
Swept the locked lilies to and fro.

With cedar paddle, scented, red,
He pushed out from the lily bed.

TORONTO

She moves to meet the centuries, her feet
All shod with emerald, and her light robe
Fringed with leaves singing in the jazel air.
Her tire is rich, not with stout battlements,
Prophets of strife, but wealthy with tall spires
All shining Godward, rare with learning's domes,
And burning with young stars that promise suns
To clasp her older brows. On her young breast
Lie linked the fair, clear pearls of many homes,—
Mighty and lovely chain, from its white strength
Hangs on her heart the awful jewel, Hope.

She moves to meet the centuries, nor lies
All languid waiting, with the murmuring kiss
Of the large waters on white, nerveless feet,
And dim, tranced gaze upon the harbour bar,
And dusk, still boughs knit over her prone head,
And rose-soft hands that idly pluck the turf,
And rose lips singing idly thro' her dream.

She hears the marching centuries which Time
Leads up the dark peaks of Eternity:
The pulses of past warriors pound in her;
The pulses of dead sages beat in her;
The pulses of dead merchants stir in her;
The roses of her young feet turn to flame,
Yet ankle-deep in tender buds of spring;

Till, with the perfumes of close forests thick
Upon her tender flesh, she to her lips
Lifts the bold answering trump, and, winding shrill
With voices of her people and her waves
Notes of quick joy, half queen, half child, she bounds

To meet the coming Time, and climbs the steps
Of the tall throne he builds upon her strand.

Toronto, joy and peace! When comes the day
Close domes of marble rich with gold leap up
From porphyry pillars to the eye-clear sky,
And when the wealthy fringes of thy robe
Sweep outward league on league, and to thee come
The years all bowed with treasures for thy house,
On lusty shoulders, still remember thee
Of thy first cradle on the lilies' lap
In the dim woods; and tho' thy diadem
Make a new sunrise, still, amid its flame,
Twine for the nursing lilies' sake the glow
Of God-like lilies round about thy brows—
Honour and Peace and sweet-breathed Charity!

THE CITY TREE

I stand within the stony, arid town,
        I gaze forever on the narrow street,
I hear forever passing up and down
        The ceaseless tramp of feet.

I know no brotherhood with far-locked woods,
        Where branches bourgeon from a kindred sap,
Where o'er mossed roots, in cool, green solitudes,
        Small silver brooklets lap.

No emerald vines creep wistfully to me
        And lay their tender fingers on my bark;
High may I toss my boughs, yet never see
        Dawn's first most glorious spark.

When to and fro my branches wave and sway,
    Answ'ring the feeble wind that faintly calls,
They kiss no kindred boughs, but touch alway
    The stones of climbing walls.

My heart is never pierced with song of bird;
    My leaves know nothing of that glad unrest
Which makes a flutter in the still woods heard
    When wild birds build a nest.

There never glance the eyes of violets up,
    Blue, into the deep splendour of my green;
Nor falls the sunlight to the primrose cup
    My quivering leaves between.

Not mine, not mine to turn from soft delight
    Of woodbine breathings, honey sweet and warm;
With kin embattled rear my glorious height
    To greet the coming storm!

Not mine to watch across the free, broad plains
    The whirl of stormy cohorts sweeping fast,
The level silver lances of great rains
    Blown onward by the blast!

Not mine the clamouring tempest to defy,
    Tossing the proud crest of my dusky leaves—
Defender of small flowers that trembling lie
    Against my barky greaves!

Not mine to watch the wild swan drift above,
    Balanced on wings that could not choose
    between
The wooing sky, blue as the eye of love,
    And my own tender green!

And yet my branches spread, a kingly sight,
    In the close prison of the drooping air;
When sun-vexed noons are at their fiery height
    My shade is broad, and there

Come city toilers, who their hour of ease
    Weave out to precious seconds as they lie
Pillowed on horny hands, to hear the breeze
    Through my great branches die.

I see no flowers, but as the children race
    With noise and clamour through the dusty street,
I see the bud of many an angel face,
    I hear their merry feet.

No violets look up, but, shy and grave,
    The children pause and lift their crystal eyes
To where my emerald branches call and wave
    As to the mystic skies.

THE DARK STAG

A startled stag, the blue-grey Night,
    Leaps down beyond black pines.
Behind—a length of yellow light—
    The hunter's arrow shines:
His moccasins are stained with red,
    He bends upon his knee,
From covering peaks his shafts are sped,
The blue mists plume his mighty head,—
    Well may the swift Night flee!

The pale, pale Moon, a snow-white doe,
  Bounds by his dappled flank:
They beat the stars down as they go,
  Like wood-bells growing rank.
The winds lift dewlaps from the ground,
  Leap from the quaking reeds;
Their hoarse bays shake the forests round,
With keen cries on the track they bound,—
  Swift, swift the dark stag speeds!

Away! his white doe, far behind,
  Lies wounded on the plain;
Yells at his flank the nimblest wind,
  His large tears fall in rain;
Like lily-pads, small clouds grow white
  About his darkling way;
From his bald nest upon the height
The red-eyed eagle sees his flight;
He falters, turns, the antlered Night,—
  The dark stag stands at bay!

His feet are in the waves of space;
  His antlers broad and dun
He lowers; he turns his velvet face
  To front the hunter, Sun;
He stamps the lilied clouds, and high
  His branches fill the west.
The lean stork sails across the sky,
The sky loon shrieks to see him die,
  The winds leap at his breast.

Roar the rent lakes as thro' the wave
  Their silver warriors plunge,
As vaults from core of crystal cave
  The strong, fierce muskallunge;

Red torches of the sumach glare,
    Fall's council-fires are lit;
The bittern, squaw-like, scolds the air;
The wild duck splashes loudly where
    The rustling rice-spears knit.

Shaft after shaft the red Sun speeds;
    Rent the stag's dappled side,
His breast, fanged by the shrill winds, bleeds,
    He staggers on the tide;
He feels the hungry waves of space
    Rush at him high and blue;
Their white spray smites his dusky face,
Swifter the Sun's fierce arrows race
    And pierce his stout heart thro'.

His antlers fall; once more he spurns
    The hoarse hounds of the day;
His blood upon the crisp blue burns,
    Reddens the mounting spray;
His branches smite the wave—with cries
    The loud winds pause and flag—
He sinks in space—red glow the skies,
The brown earth crimsons as he dies,
    The strong and dusky stag.

from MALCOLM'S KATIE

...I heard him tell
How the first field upon his farm was ploughed.
He and his brother Reuben, stalwart lads,
Yoked themselves, side by side, to the new plough;

Their weaker father, in the grey of life—
But rather the wan age of poverty
Than many winters—in large, gnarled hands
The plunging handles held; with mighty strains
They drew the ripping beak through knotted sod,
Thro' tortuous lanes of blackened, smoking stumps,
And past great, flaming brush-heaps, sending out
Fierce summers, beating on their swollen brows.
O such a battle! had we heard of serfs
Driven to like hot conflict with the soil,
Armies had marched and navies swiftly sailed
To burst their gyves. But here's the little point—
The polished diamond pivot on which spins
The wheel of difference—they OWNED the soil,
And fought for love—dear love of wealth and power—
And honest ease and fair esteem of men.
One's blood heats at it!

Part I
lines 70 - 90

from MALCOLM'S KATIE

So shanties grew
Other than his amid the blackened stumps;
And children ran with little twigs and leaves
And flung them, shouting, on the forest pyres
Where burned the forest kings; and in the glow
Paused men and women when the day was done.
There the lean weaver ground anew his axe,
Nor backward looked upon the vanished loom,
But forward to the ploughing of his fields,

And to the rose of plenty in the cheeks
Of wife and children; nor heeded much the pangs
Of the roused muscles tuning to new work.
The pallid clerk looked on his blistered palms
And sighed and smiled, but girded up his loins
And found new vigour as he felt new hope.
The lab'rer with trained muscles, grim and grave,
Looked at the ground, and wondered in his soul
What joyous anguish stirred his darkened heart
At the mere look of the familiar soil,
and found his answer in the words, *"Mine own!"*

Part II
lines 212-231

from MALCOLM'S KATIE

There came a morn the Moon of Falling Leaves
…"Esa! esa! shame upon you Pale Face!
Shame upon you, Moon of Evil Witches!
Have you killed the happy, laughing Summer?
Have you slain the mother of the flowers
With your icy spells of might and magic?
Have you laid her dead within my arms?
Wrapped her, mocking, in a rainbow blanket?
Drowned her in the frost-mist of your anger?
She is gone a little way before me
Gone an arrow's flight beyond my vision.
She will turn again and come to meet me
With the ghosts of all the stricken flowers,
In a blue mist round her shining tresses,
In a blue smoke in her naked forests.
She will linger, kissing all the branches;

She will linger, touching all the places,
Bare and naked, with her golden fingers,
Saying, 'Sleep and dream of me, my children;
Dream of me, the mystic Indian Summer.' "

Part II
lines 110 - 127

from MALCOLM'S KATIE

In this shrill moon the scouts of Winter ran
From the ice-belted north, and whistling shafts
Struck maple and struck sumach, and a blaze
Ran swift from leaf to leaf, from bough to bough,
Till round the forest flashed a belt of flame,
And inward licked its tongues of red and gold
To the deep-crannied inmost heart of all.
Roused the still heart—but all too late, too late!
Too late the branches, welded fast with leaves,
Tossed, loosened, to the winds; too late the Sun
Poured his last vigour to the deep, dark cells
Of the dim wood. The keen two-bladed Moon
Of Falling Leaves rolled up on crested mists,
And where the lush, rank boughs had foiled the Sun
In his red prime, her pale, sharp fingers crept
After the wind and felt about the moss,
And seemed to pluck from shrinking twig and stem
The burning leaves, while groaned the shuddering
wood.

Part II
lines 50 - 68

from MALCOLM'S KATIE

From his far wigwam sprang the strong North Wind
And rushed with war-cry down the steep ravines,
And wrestled with the giants of the woods;
And with his ice-club beat the swelling crests
Of the deep watercourses into death;
And with his chill foot froze the whirling leaves
Of dun and gold and fire in icy banks;
And smote the tall reeds to the hardened earth,
And sent his whistling arrows o'er the plains,
Scattering the lingering herds; and sudden paused,
When he had frozen all the running streams,
And hunted with his war-cry all the things
That breathed about the woods, or roamed the bleak,
Bare prairies swelling to the mournful sky.

...High grew the snow beneath the low hung sky,
And all was silent in the wilderness.

                                    Part IV
                                  lines 1 - 14
                                  lines 34 - 35

from MALCOLM'S KATIE

"Nations are not immortal. Is there now
One nation throned upon the sphere of earth
That walked with the first gods and with them saw
The budding world unfold its slow-leaved flower?
Nay, it is hardly theirs to leave behind
Ruins so eloquent that the hoary sage

Can lay his hand upon their stones and say"
'These once were thrones!'

      "The lean, lank lion peals
His midnight thunders over lone, red plains,
Long-ridged and crested on their dusty waves
With fires from moons red-hearted as the sun,
And deep re-thunders all the earth to him;
For, far beneath the flame-flecked, shifting sands,
Below the roots of palms, and under stones
Of younger ruins, thrones, towers and cities
Honeycomb the earth. The high, solemn walls
Of hoary ruins—their foundings all unknown
But to the round-eyed worlds that walk
In the blank paths of Space and blanker Chance—
At whose stones young mountains wonder, and the seas'
New-silvering, deep-set valleys pause and gaze—
Are reared upon old shrines whose very gods
Were dreams to the shrine-builders of a time
They caught in far-off flashes—as the child
Half thinks he can remember how one came
And took him in her hand and showed him that,
He thinks, she called the sun.

Part IV
lines 58 - 86

from MALCOLM'S KATIE

"Nations immortal? Where the well-trimmed lamps
Of long-past ages? When Time seemed to pause
On smooth, dust-blotted graves that, like the tombs
Of monarchs, held dead bones and sparkling gems,

She saw no glimmer on the hideous ring
Of the black clouds; no stream of sharp, clear light
From those great torches passed into the black
Of deep oblivion. She seemed to watch, but she
Forgot her long-dead nations. When she stirred
Her vast limbs in the dawn that forced its fire
Up the black East, and saw the imperious red
Burst over virgin dews and budding flowers,
She still forgot her mouldered thrones and kings,
Her sages and their torches and their gods,
And said, 'This is my birth—my primal day!'
She dreamed new gods, and reared them other shrines,
Planted young nations, smote a feeble flame
From sunless flint, re-lit the torch of mind.
Again she hung her cities on the hills,
Built her rich towers, crowned her kings again;
And with the sunlight on her awful wings
Swept round the flowery cestus of the earth,
And said, 'I build for Immortality!'
Her vast hand reared her towers, her shrines, her thrones;
The ceaseless sweep of her tremendous wings
Still beat them down and swept their dust abroad.
Her iron fingers wrote on mountain sides
Her deeds and prowess, and her own soft plume
Wore down the hills. Again drew darkly on
A night of deep forgetfulness; once more
Time seemed to pause upon forgotten graves;
Once more a young dawn stole into her eyes;
Again her broad wings stirred, and fresh, clear airs
Blew the great clouds apart; again she said,
'This is my birth—my deeds and handiwork
Shall be immortal!' Thus and so dream on
Fooled nations, and thus dream their dullard sons,
Naught is immortal save immortal—Death!"

Part IV
lines 103 - 141

from MALCOLM'S KATIE

Said the high hill, in the morning, "Look on me!
Behold, sweet earth, sweet sister sky, behold
The red flames on my peaks, and how my pines
Are cressets of pure gold, my quarried scars
Of black crevasse and shadow-filled canyon
Are traced in silver mist. Now on my breast
Hang the soft purple fringes of the night;
Close to my shoulder droops the weary moon,
Dove-pale, into the crimson surf the sun
Drives up before his prow; and blackly stands
On my slim, loftiest peak an eagle with
His angry eyes set sunward, while his cry
Falls fiercely back from all my ruddy heights,
And his bald eaglets, in their bare, broad nest,
Shrill pipe their angry echoes: 'Sun, arise,
And show me that pale dove beside her nest,
Which I shall strike with piercing beak and tear
With iron talons for my hungry young.'

"And that mild dove, secure for yet a space,
Half wakened, turns her ringed and glossy neck
To watch the dawn's ruby pulsing on my breast,
And see the first bright golden motes slip down
The gnarled trunks about her leaf-deep nest,
Nor sees nor fears the eagle on the peak."

Part V
lines 1 - 24

from MALCOLM'S KATIE

Who curseth Sorrow knows her not at all.
Dark matrix she, from which the human soul

Has its last birth; whence it, with misty thews
Close knitted in her blackness, issues out
Strong for immortal toil up such great heights
As crown o'er crown rise through Eternity.
Without the loud, deep clamour of her wail,
The iron of her hands, the biting brine
Of her black tears, the soul, but lightly built
Of indeterminate spirit, like a mist
Would lapse to chaos in soft, gilded dreams,
As mists fade in the gazing of the sun.
Sorrow, dark mother of the soul, arise!

Part VI
lines 1 - 13

from MALCOLM'S KATIE

For love, once set within a lover's breast,
Has its own sun, its own peculiar sky,
All one great daffodil, on which do lie
The sun, the moon, the stars, all seen at once
And never setting, but all shining straight
Into the faces of the trinity—
The one beloved, the lover, and sweet love.

Part II
lines 185 - 191

from THE ROSE OF A NATION'S THANKS

A Welcome? Oh yes, 'tis a kindly word, but why will
they plan and prate
Of feasting and speeches and such small things, while the
wives, and mothers wait?
Plan as ye will, and do as ye will, but think of the hunger
and thirst
In the hearts that wait; and do as ye will, but lend us our
laddies first!

A Welcome? Why, what do you mean by that, when the
very stones must sing
As our men march over them home again; the walls of
the city ring
With the thunder of throats and the tramp and tread of
feet that rush and run?—
I think in my heart that the very trees must shout for the
bold work done!
Why, what would ye have? There is not a lad that treads
in the gallant ranks
Who does not already bear on his breast the Rose of a
Nations' Thanks!

A Welcome? There is not a babe in the breast won't
spring at the roll of the drum
That heralds them home—the keen, long cry in the air
of "They come! They come!"
And what of it all if ye bade them wade knee-deep in a
wave of wine,
And tossed tall torches, and arched the town in garlands
of maple and pine?
All dust in the wind of a woman's cry as she snatches
from the ranks
Her boy who bears on his bold young breast the Rose of
a Nation's Thanks!

stanzas 1 - 3

OLD SPOOKSES' PASS

We'd chanced thet night on a pootyish lot
    With a tol'ble show uv tall, sweet grass—
We wus takin' Speredo's drove across
    The Rockies, by way uv "Old Spookses' Pass"—
An' a mite uv a crick went crinklin' down,
    Like a "pocket" bust in the rocks overhead,
Consid'able shrunk by the summer drought
    Tew a silver streak in its gravelly bed.
"Twus a fairish spot fur tew camp a' night;
    An' chipper I felt, tho' sort uv skeered
Thet them two cowboys, with only me,
    Couldn't boss three thousand head uv a herd.
I took the fust uv the watch myself;
    An' es the red sun down the mountains sprang,
I rolled a fresh quid, an' got on the back
    Uv my peart lettle chunk uv a tough mustang.
An' Possum Billy wus sleepin' sound
    Es only a cowboy knows how tew sleep;
An' Tommy's snores would hev made a old
    Buffalo bull feel kind o' cheap.
Wal, pard, I reckon thar's no sech time
    Fur dwindlin' a chap in his own conceit
Es when them mountains an' awful stars
    Jest hark tew the tramp uv his mustang's feet.

It 'pears tew me thet them solemn hills
    Beckon them stars so big an' calm,
An' whisper, "Make tracks this way, my friends,
    We've ringed in here a specimen man;
He's here alone, so we'll take a look
    Thru his ganzy an' vest, an' his blood an' bone,
An' post ourselves es tew whether his heart
    Is *flesh*, or a rotten, made-up stone."

An' it's often seemed, on a midnight watch,
    When the mountains blackened the dry, brown
    sod
Thet a chap, if he shet his eyes, might grip
    The great, kind hand uv his Father God.
I rode round the herd at a sort uv walk;
    The shadders cum stealin' thick an' black
I'd just got tew leave tew thet thar chunk
    Uv a mustang tew keep in the proper track.

Ever see'd a herd ringed in at night?
    Wal, it's sort uv cur'us—the watchin' sky,
The howl uv coyotes, a great black mass
    With here an' thar the gleam uv a eye
An' the white uv a horn, an' now an' then
    An old bull liftin' his shaggy head
With a beller like a broke-up thunder growl,
    An, the summer lightnin', quick an' red,
Twistin' an turnin' amid the stars,
    Silent as snakes at play in the grass,
An' plungin' thair fangs in the bare old skulls
    Uv the mountains frownin' above the Pass;
An' all so still, thet the leetle crick,
    Twinklin' and crinklin' frum stone tew stone,
Grows louder an' louder an' fills the air
    With a cur'us sort uv a singin' tone.
It ain't no matter wherever ye be,—
    I'll 'low it's a cur'us sort uv case
Whar thar's runnin' water, it's sure tew speak
    Uv folks tew home an' the old home place;

An' yer bound tew listen an' hear it talk,
    Es yer mustang crunches the dry, bald sod,
Fur I reckon the hills an' stars an' crick
    Are all uv 'em preachers sent by God.

An, them mountains talk tew a chap this way:
     "Climb, if ye can, ye degenerate cuss!"
An' the stars smile down on a man, an' say,
     "Cum higher, poor critter, cum up tew us!"

Old Spookses' Pass
stanzas 4 - 11

from THE KING'S GARMENTS

"For Law immutable hath one decree,
'No deed of good, no deed of ill can die;
All must ascend unto my loom and be
Woven for man in lasting tapestry,
Each soul his own.'

lines 63 - 68

EPILOGUE

At the turn of the century, John W. Garvin held the position of Inspector of public schools in Peterborough, Ontario. This post was relinquished in order to pursue a career in the insurance field in Toronto. It is not known when Garvin first became fascinated with the poetry of Isabella Valancy Crawford, but Catherine Crawford Humphrey tells us that Garvin's interest took him to 57 John Street in Toronto. There he found, much to his horror, poems and old manuscripts were being used to kindle fires in the third-floor flat of the Stuart home, the very rooms in which the poet lived during the last years of her life. He piled what remained into cartons. These papers can now be found in the Lorne Pierce Collection, Queen's University, Kingston, Ontario. Garvin then contacted Stephen Walter Crawford, Isabella's brother and with his help, *The Collected Poems of Isabella Valancy Crawford* were published in 1905.

In 1912, John Garvin married Amelia Beers Warnock (Katherine Hale) of Galt, Ontario. Katherine Hale, a poet, and literary critic of the Toronto *Mail and Empire,* shared her husband's admiration for Crawford. In 1923, Hale published *Isabella Valancy Crawford, Makers of Canadian Literature* series (Toronto: Ryerson). It was a small volume, but it contained biographical information, an appreciation of Crawford's work, a miscellany of her poetry, and an invaluable bibliography.

During the years immediately following Crawford's death, her poetry appeared in several anthologies: *The Canadian Birthday Book*, edited by "Seranus" (Toronto: C. Blackett Robinson, 1887); *Songs of the Great Dominion*, edited by W.D. Lighthall (London: W. Scott, 1889); and *Younger American Poets 1830-90*, edited by Douglas Sladen (New York: Cassell, 1891).

Since that time, her work has been reprinted in numerous major Canadian anthologies, including *The Oxford Book of Canadian Verse*, edited by A.J.M. Smith (Toronto: Oxford Press, 1967). For years, *Shorter Poems*, edited by W.J. Alexander, was a prescribed textbook for English courses in Ontario high schools, and this volume contained several of Crawford's poems.

In 1972, the University of Toronto Press, in its Nineteenth-Century Reprint Series, published a re-issue of the 1905 edition, *The Collected Poems of Isabella Valancy Crawford*—this time with an introduction by James Reaney. Other publications are listed in this volume, under *Works of Isabella Valancy Crawford*.

Her writing has been the subject of a number of M.A. and doctoral theses, and many scholarly articles have been printed in Canadian literary journals. Serafina Penny Petrone's doctoral dissertation, *The Imaginative Achievement of Isabella Valancy Crawford*, University of Alberta, 1977, is particularly praiseworthy.

In 1989, Robert Allan Burns, University of Guam, published a paper "The Poet in Her Time: Isabella Valancy Crawford's Social, Economic and Political Views" in *Studies in Canadian Literature* in which he presented a critical analysis of her work within that context.

Among the Canadian literary luminaries who have acclaimed Crawford's poetry are: Northrop Frye, Roy

Daniells, Dorothy Livesay, Clara Thomas, Fred Cogswell, James Reaney and Robert Fulford.

In 1977, on May 6, 7 and 8, the fifth symposium in the University of Ottawa Symposia series, sponsored by the Department of English, studied the creative writings of Crawford. Papers presented by North American writers at this symposium were published: *The Isabella Valancy Crawford Symposium*, edited and with an introduction by Frank M. Teirney (Ottawa: University of Ottawa Press, 1979).

On September 9th, 1983, the Historic Sites and Monuments Board of Canada, unveiled a commemorative plaque in Scott's Plains Park in Peterborough, Ontario, on the banks of the Otonabee River, immediately behind the location of the Crawfords' first Peterborough residence (now a T. Eaton store).

The house where Dr. Crawford died is still standing, on the south-west corner of George and Edinburgh Streets in Peterborough. So, too, is the little wooden house in Paisley. Will these structures survive? I think not. The house at the corner of King and John Streets where Isabella died has been demolished. However, a short distance away at the foot of John Street, 315 Front Street West, on property made available by the Royal Bank of Canada, a small park has been named Isabella Valancy Crawford Park with a commemorative plaque unveiled by the Toronto Historical Board on May 21, 1992.

It is of interest to note several inaccuracies. On the Toronto plaque Old Spookses' Pass is incorrectly spelled Old Spookeses' Pass. On the Paisley plaque, Isabella's birthdate, generally accepted as Dcember 25, 1850 is given as "about 1846."

On the programme for the Peterborough plaque unveiling ceremony, a photograph of the poet's gravestone has an incorrect inscription printed beneath it, and reads: Poet by the Grace of God instead of Poet by the Gift of God. Thus further confusion is perpetuated.

Despite recognition, the poet remains strangely uncelebrated. With the emergence of a universally-acknowledged, unique Canadian literature, perhaps Crawford will be given the title she merits—that of Canada's first woman poet.

NOTES

Author's Preface

1   J.W. Garvin, *The Collected Poems of Isabella Valancy Crawford*, (Toronto: Wm. Briggs, 1905), p. 1.

2   Serafina (Penny) Petrone, *The Imaginative Achievement of Isabella Valancy Crawford*. Unpublished Ph.D. thesis,University of Alberta, 1977, p. 1.

3   Dorothy Farmiloe, *Isabella Valancy Crawford, The Life and the Legends*, (Ottawa: Tecumseh Press, 1983) p. xiv.

4   1861 Census, Elderslie Township (Reel C 1011), p. 8.

5   1871 Census, Peterborough, Archives of Ontario, (Reel C-640), p. 16.

6   1881 Census, City of Toronto, Archives of Ontario.

7   Lorne Pierce Collection, Douglas Library, Queen's University, Kingston, Ontario.

8   Katherine Hale (Mrs. John Garvin), *Isabella Valancy Crawford*, Makers of Canadian Literature Series, (Toronto: Ryerson, 1923)

9   Crawford Manuscripts, Lorne Pierce Collection (L.P.C.), Douglas Library, Queen's University, Kingston, Ontario

10   Hale, op. cit. p. 3.

11   John Garvin, *Who Was Who in Canada 1875 - 1937*, (Toronto: Murray Publishing, 1938)

12   *Collected Poems, Isabella Valancy Crawford*, Introduction by James Reancy, (Toronto, University of Toronto Press, 1972), p. xi.

13   The Oxford Book of Canadian Verse, Introduction by A.J.M.
      Smith, (Toronto: Oxford University Press, 1970), p. xxx.
14   Petrone, op. cit.
15   General Register of Ireland 1846 (Dublin Almanac), Four
      Courts Building, Dublin.
16   Elizabeth Galvin, *"Isabella Valancy Crawford - Poet"*, *Portraits:*
      Peterborough Area Women, Past and Present, ed. Gail Corbett,
            (Peterborough: Woodbine, 1975), p. 82.
17   Elizabeth Galvin, "Isabella Valancy Crawford - Poet, by the Gift
            of God," *Kawartha Heritage,* Proceedings of the Kawartha
            Conference 1981, eds. A.O.C. Cole and Jean Murray Cole,
            (Peterborough: 1981), p. 136.
18   Peterborough Historical Society, Bulletin No. 163, January
      1988 Martha Tancock, "Monodrama Recalls Tragic Life of
      Early Canadian Poet", *Peterborough Examiner*, January 23,
      1987, p. 14.

Dublin

1   Catherine Crawford Humphrey, *Biographical Sketch of Isabella
     Valancy Crawford*, Ch. I, p. 1.
2   General Register of Ireland, 1846, Four Courts, Dublin.
3   Humphrey, op. cit. Ch. 1, p. 2.
4   Ibid.
5   Letter received by me from the Royal College of Surgeons of
     England, dated April 7, 1987: "Stephen Dennis Crawford did
     attend one class in clinical medicine in the winter of 1823-33 at
     Edinburgh University."
6   Humphrey, op. cit. Ch.1. p. 7 (e).
7   Autobiographical sketch written by Isabella Valancy Crawford
     for Mrs. J.W. F. Harrison (Seranus) who was on the editorial
     staff of *The Week* cl. 1885, (*Elsie Pomeroy Collection*, Mount
     Allison University Archives (acc. 5001), Sackville, New Brunswick.
8   Edmund Curtis, *A History of Ireland*, (London: Methuen, 1936).
9   Humphrey, op. cit. Ch. 1, p. 2.
10   Humphrey, op. cit. Ch. 1, p. 4.
11   Ibid.

12 Provincial Secretary, Canada West, April 1. 1857, Numbered
Correspondence Files (RG 5, C 1, Vol. 507, File 561 of 1857).
13 P.S.O. Correspondence Register (File 1742 of 1857).

Paisley

1 "Paisley in the Early Days", *Paisley Advocate*, The
Commemorative Issue, February 20, 1890.
2 Instrument #39, Walkerton Registry Office. Crown to Sydney
Crawford.
3 Humphrey, op. cit. Ch.I, p. 4 (7h).
4 Humphrey, op. cit. Ch.I, p. 4 (8).
5 The Ledgers and Account Books of Dr. John Hutchison,
Hutchison House Museum Archives, Peterborough, Ontario.
Courtesy of Cindy Paul-Girdwood, Curator.
6 "Professions", *Paisley Advocate*, op. cit.
7 Norman Robertson, *The History of the County of Bruce*. (Wm.
Briggs, 1906), p. 86.
8 "Paisley in the Early Days", *Paisley Advocate*, op. cit.
9 Humphrey, op. cit. Ch. II. p. 3 (7b).
10 1861 Census Elderslie Township (Reel C-1011, p.8).
11 "Education", *Paisley Advocate*, op. cit.
12 "Our Churches", *Paisley Advocate*, op. cit.
13 "Antrim" (Mrs. Annie Sutherland, granddaughter of Samuel
Rowe). "Old Paisley Landmark Once Writer's Home", *The Free
Press*, London, Ontario (July 2, 1927).
14 Thomas O'Hagan, *Gardiner Scrapbooks*, Hamilton Public
Library, Vol. 117, p. 77.
15 Maud Miller Wilson, *Isabella Valancy Crawford*, a biographical
sketch in L.P.C., typescript, n.d., n.p. Wilson was the wife of
McFarlane Wilson, proprietor of The China Hall on George
Street in Peterborough in the early twentieth century.
16 "Antrim", op. cit.
17 Ibid
18 Humphrey, op. cit. Ch. II, p. 2. (5).
19 Mary F. Martin, *"The Short Life of Isabella Valancy Crawford"*,
Dalhousie Review, 52 (Autumn 1972) p. 393.

20   "Antrim", op. cit.
21   Wilson, op. cit.
22   "Professions", *Paisley Advocate*, op. cit.
23   Courtesy of Eric Parker, Paisley, Ontario.
24   Ibid.
25   The Paisley Advocate (January 11, 1867) p. 1. Courtesy of Eric Parker, Paisley, Ontario.

Lakefield

1   Samuel Strickland, *Twenty-seven years in Canada West: or, The experiences of an early settler,* (2 vols. London, 1853). Catherine Parr Traill, *The backwoods of Canada: being letters of the wife of an emigrant officer: illustrative of the domestic econo my of British America* (London 1836). Susanna Moodie, *Roughing it in the bush: or, Forest Life in Canada* (London 1852)
2   Hale, op. cit. p. 3.
3   Martin, op. cit. p. 392.
4   Frank Dobbin, *Peterborough Medical Association 1921-22.* Dobbin was compiling a history of medical men in the Peterborough area. It exists in manuscript form at the Peterborough Centennial Museum.
5   Baldwin Collection, Metro. Toronto Library. Courtesy of Prof. Michael Peterman, Trent University, Peterborough, Ontario.
6   Sherin Papers (ref. 71-002), Trent University Archives.
7   Christ Church Cemetery Records, North Douro, Courtesy of Susan Twist, Lakefield, Ontario.
8   Traill Family Collection, National Archives, (M.G. 29 D 81) pp. 10231 & 10232.
9   Martin, op. cit. p. 393. Notes sent to Martin by Mary Traill, based on information contained in the Atwood Scrapbook.
10   Hale, op. cit. p. 12.
11   Martin, op. cit. p. 392. Letter of John Twist to Martin.
12   Traill Family Papers—National Archives. Letter written by Catherine Parr Traill to her daughter, Annie Atwood. Courtesy of Prof. M. Peterman, Trent University.

13   Unpublished diary of Catherine Parr Traill. Courtesy of Susan Twist of Lakefield.
14   Ibid.
15   Ibid.
16   *Susanna Moodie, Letters of a Lifetime*, eds. Ballstadt, Hopkins and Peterman, (Toronto: University of Toronto Press, 1985). Letter of July 10, 1865.
17   Martin, op. cit. p. 393, notes from Mary Traill.
18   Ibid.
19   Frances Stewart, *Our Forest Home*, (Gazette Printing 1902), pp. 283-284.
20   Martin, op. cit. p. 393.
21   Crawford manuscripts, L.P.C.
22   F.H. Dobbin, *Our Old Home Town*, (Toronto: J.M. Dent & Sons 1943)
23   Traill Papers, The National Archives, Ottawa. Letter of Catherine Parr Traill to her daughter, Kate. Courtesy of Prof. M. Peterman, Trent University.
24   Crawford manuscripts, L.P.C.
25   Dr. Raymore Scott, "The Pioneer Doctors", *Peterborough, Land of Shining Waters*, (Toronto: University of Toronto Press 1967).
26   Wilson, op. cit.
27   Public Record Office, Kew, Richmond, Surrey, England. Record of Officers' Services (ADM 196/8 p. 218).

Peterborough

1   "Jeanette"—"Great Poetess Buried in Little Lake Cemetery", *Peterborough Examiner*, March 20, 1934.
2   Dr. Thos. W. Poole, *A Sketch of the Early Settlement and Subsequent Progress of the Town of Peterborough* etc. (Peterborough C.W.: Peterborough Review, 1867).
3   F.H. Dobbin, op. cit.
4   Archives of St. John's Anglican Church, Peterborough, Ontario.
5   Wilson, op. cit.
6   Sister Patricia O'Brien, "Isabella Valancy Crawford",

Peterborough, Land of Shining Waters, published by City and County of Peterborough, (Toronto: University of Toronto Press 1967) pp. 379-383.

7   Peterborough Directories, Centennial Museum. Ryan's Building, later known at Green's Terraces, both located at 324 Water St.

8   Hale, op. cit. p. 114.

9   Ibid.

10 Humphrey, op. cit. Ch. IV, p. 8 (8).

11 Farmiloe, op. cit. p. 46

12 Crawford manuscript, L.P.C.

13 "Jeanette" op. cit.

14 Ibid.

15 Ibid.

16 Dorothy Livesay, "Tennyson's Daughter or Wilderness Child", *Journal Canadian Fiction II*, 3 (Summer 1973) pp. 161-167

17 Farmiloe, op. cit. pp. 37-38.

18 Petrone, *The Imaginative Achievement of Isabella Valancy Crawford*, unpublished Ph.D. thesis, University of Alberta 1977. p. 21

19 "Jeanette", op. cit.

Toronto

1   *The Collected Poems of Isabella Valancy Crawford*, edited by John Garvin, (Toronto: Wm: Briggs 1905).

2   Crawford's signature appears in the Mechanic's Institute Register No. 1232.

3   Crawford manuscript, L.P.C.

4   Dorothy Farmiloe, *Isabella Valancy Crawford, The Life and and the Legends*, (Ottawa: Tecumseh Press 1983), p. 83.

5   C.P. Mulvaney, *Toronto, Past and Present* (Toronto: 1884).

6   Petrone, *The Imaginative Achievement of Isabella Valancy Crawford*, unpublished Ph.D. thesis, University of Alberta 1977, p. 375.

7   John Garvin, *A Standard Dictionary of Canadian Biography*, (Toronto: 1938) p. 75.

8   Crawford manuscripts, L.P.C.

9   Ibid.

10 "Jeanette", op. cit.

11 E.J. Hathaway, *The Canadian Magazine*, October 5, 1895.

12 *London Spectator*, October 18, 1884.

13 Letter reproduced in facsimile p. 5. 1905 edition of *Collected Poems of Isabella Valancy Crawford*, ed. J. Garvin.

14 *The Globe*, June 3-9, 1884.

15 "The Encouragement of Native Literature", *The Varsity*, January 23, 1886, p. 116.

16 Hale, op. cit. pp. 113-114. Also—"...in 1898 a considerable store of unsold copies of what may be called the 'author's edition' (although how many is not definitely known at this late date) was found and, after being rebound in light blue cloth boards, with lettering and floral design on the face in silver, and letter on the back, also in silver, put on the market by William Briggs."

17 Maud Miller Wilson, L.P.C

18 L.P.C. manuscriipts in handwriting identified as that of Sydney Crawford.

19 Bruce West, *Toronto*, "An Era of Progress 1858-85", (Toronto: Doubleday 1967) p. 172.

20 *Arcturus*, February 19, 1887, p. 84, published posthumously.

21 Wilson, op. cit.

22 Hale, op. cit. p. 12.

23 Hale, op. cit. p. 13.

24 Petrone, op. cit. p. 15.

25 Hale, op. cit. p. 15.

26 *Gardiner Scrapbooks*, Special Collections Department, Vol. 117, p. 77, Hamilton Public Library.

WORKS OF
ISABELLA VALANCY CRAWFORD

Old Spookses' Pass, Malcolm's Katie and Other Poems.
Toronto: James Bain and Son, 1884
The Collected Poems of Isabella Valancy Crawford.
Toronto: W. Briggs, 1905.
Edited by John W. Garvin with an introduction by Ethelwyn Wetherald.
Isabella Valancy Crawford.
Toronto: Ryerson Press, 1923.
Katherine Hale.
(In some listings the same volume has the author's name as Amelia Beers Warnock.)
Collected Poems Isabella Valancy Crawford.
Toronto: University of Toronto Press, 1972.
The 1905 edition reprinted in facsimile, with an introduction by James Reaney.
Selected Stories of Isabella Valancy Crawford.
Ottawa: University of Ottawa Press, 1975.
Edited and with an introduction by Penny Petrone.
Fairy Tales of Isabella Valancy Crawford.
Ottawa: Borealis Press, 1977.
Edited by Penny Petrone.
Hugh and Ion.
Ottawa: Borealis Press, 1977.
Edited, with introduction and notes by Glen Clever.
The Halton Boys.
Ottawa: Borealis Press, 1979.
Edited by and with an introduction by Frank M. Tierney.

SELECTED BIBLIOGRAPHY

"Antrim" Mrs. Annie Sutherland, "Old Paisley Landmark Once
　　Writer's Home", *The London Free Press*, 2 July 1927.

Ballstadt, Carl et al., (eds.). Susanna Moodie: *Letters of a Lifetime*.
　　Toronto: University of Toronto Press, 1985.

Burns, Robert Alan. "The Poet in Her Time: Isabella Valancy
　　Crawford's Social, Economic, and Political Views." *Studies in
　　Canadian Literature* 14 (1) (1989) 30 - 53.

Careless, J.M.S. *Toronto to 1918: An Illustrated History*. Toronto:
　　James Lorimer, 1984.

Cole, A.O.C. and Jean Murray Cole (eds). *Illustrated Historical Atlas
　　Peterborough County 1825 - 1875*, published by The
　　Peterborough Historical Atlas Foundation Inc. 1975.

Curtis, Edmund. *A History of Ireland*. London: Methuen, 1936.

Dendy, William. *Lost Toronto*. Toronto: Oxford University Press, 1978.

Dobbin, Francis Hincks. *Our Old Home Town*. Toronto: J.M. Dent
　　& Sons, 1943.

Peterborough Medical Association, 1921 - 22. Unpublished manu-
　　script at the Peterborough Centennial Museum.

Farmiloe, Dorothy. *Isabella Valancy Crawford: The Life and the
　　Legends*. Ottawa: Tecumseh Press, 1983.

"I.V. Crawford, the Growing Legend", *Canadian Literature*,
　　No. 81, Summer 1979, 143-47.

Glazebrook, G.P. deT. *Life in Ontario: A Social History*. Toronto:
　　University of Toronto Press, 1968.

Hale, Katherine. "Isabella Valancy Crawford," *Makers of Canadian
　　Literature Series*. Toronto: Ryerson, 1923.

"Isabella Valancy Crawford 1850 - 1887" *Leading Canadian Poets*, Toronto: Ryerson c 1948, 63 - 70.

"Jeanette" "Great Poetess Buried in Little Lake Cemetery", *Peterborough Examiner*, 20 March 1934.

Kidd, Martha Ann. *Peterborough's Architectural Heritage*, Peterborough Architectureal Advisory Committee, 1978.

LaBranche, Bill. *Peterborough Scrapbook: A Pictorial History of the City of Peterborough 1825 - 1975*. Peterborough Review, 1975.

Livesay, Dorothy. "Isabella Valancy Crawford", *Dictionary of Canadian Biography*, Vol. 11. Toronto: University of Toronto Press, 1982, 212 - 214.

Martin, Mary. "The Short Life of Isabella Valancy Crawford", *Dalhousie Review* 52, Autumn 1972, 390 - 401.

"Nathaway Nan". *Yesteryear at Young's Point: Where the Kawarthas Began*. Renfrew: Customs Press, 1975.

O'Brien, Sister Patricia. "Isabella Valancy Crawford", *Peterborough: Land of Shining Waters*. Published by the City and County of Peterborough. Toronto: University of Toronto Press, 1967.

Petrone, Serafina Penny. *The Imaginative Achievement of Isabella Valancy Crawford*. Unpublished doctoral thesis, The University of Alberta, 1977.

"In Search of Isabella Valancy Crawford", *The Crawford Symposium*, Frank M. Tierney (ed.). Ottawa: University of Ottawa Press, 1979.

Poole, Dr. Thos. W. *A Sketch of the Early Settlement and Subsequent Progress of the Town of Peterborough, and of Each Township in the County of Peterborough*. Peterborough C.W.: Peterborough Review, 1867.

Robertson, Norman. *The History of the County of Bruce*. Toronto: Wm. Briggs, 1906.

Ross, Catherine, "Isabella Valancy Crawford and 'this clanging world' ", *Kawartha Heritage*, A.O.C. Cole and Jean Murray Cole (eds.). Peterborough Historical Atlas Foundation, 1981.

"Isabella Valancy Crawford", *Oxford Companion to Canadian Literature*. Toronto: Oxford University Press, 1983.

Stewart, Francis. *Our Forest Home*. Toronto: 1889.

Tierney, Frank M. (ed.). *The Isabella Valancy Crawford Symposium*. Ottawa: University of Ottawa Press, 1979.

Twist, John. "The Restoration of Christ Church, Lakefield". *Through the Years in Douro*, J. Alex Edmison (ed.). Published by The Centennial Committee of the Township of Douro, 1967.

Wilson, Maud Wheeler. "Isabella Valancy Crawford". Typescript, Lorne Pierce Collection, Queen's University archives.
The Globe, April 15, 1905 and April 22, 1905.

Young, Aileen. "The Strickland Family", *Through the Years in Douro*, J. Alex Edmison (ed.). Published by The Centennial Committee of the Township of Douro.

ABOUT THE AUTHOR

Elizabeth McNeill Galvin was born in Kitchener and grew up in the Ottawa Valley. Her poetry has appeared in anthologies and magazines including *Canadian Forum* and *Toronto Life*. She has a chapbook "The Shuttered Door" published by *Fiddlehead Poetry Books*. As well, Galvin has produced videos, written script and contributed to the publication for children "If I Had A Camel" (*Mayapple Press*, 1988). She lives with her husband, Clare (also a writer), and their little dog, Prudence Felicity, on the shores of Lake Chemong in Ennismore Township.